Illuminations

Illuminations

Expressions of the Personal Spiritual Experience

EDITED BY Mark L. Tompkins AND Jennifer McMahon

CELESTIAL ARTS
Berkeley | Toronto

as i nourished my
soul,

my heart began to

flourish.

For all the people around the world who were moved
to submit material for this book, whether it was included or not.
Without you there would be no *Illuminations*.
May your paths be rich in joy.

OPPOSITE:

Flourish

Michele Renée Ledoux, USA
INFLUENCE: EXTRAORDINARINESS OF THE ORDINARY

FACING TITLE PAGE:

Flying Ganges

Thomas Fuhs, USA
INFLUENCE: MULTIFAITH, DEVOUT YOGI

Contents

Paloma

Luis Vera Prendes, Mexico
INFLUENCE: CHRISTIANITY

Preface

The idea that lead to *Illuminations* kept returning, floating up into my consciousness until it became a desire, then an intention, then a book (with lots of small miracles in between). While the specific genesis of the concept is lost in the slipperiness of memory, it dates back to the time I began to seriously study religions, spiritual paths, and their effects on the world.

This study was soon influencing my photography, leading me to capture images of faith paths rather than of my previous mountain passes. However, in seeking to photograph Buddhism, I found I was actually photographing Buddhists; in seeking to photograph Hindu rituals, I was actually photographing people practicing their faith.

It was in connecting with these people that a subtle, but important, shift in interest occurred: for example, from, what is Judaism? to, what is it like to be someone within the Jewish faith?—particularly from the perspective of those who have looked at this question themselves and made a deliberate choice.

In order to capture the essence of an individual within a faith path, rather than the doctrine of that faith path, we adopted the following structure for the book:

First, focus on the questions that arise about spirituality, and how they shape peoples' beliefs. This is, in turn, inseparably intertwined with how these questions begin, such as the effect of life's joys, crises, and concerns.

Second, except as an adjunct to the questioning process, exclude descriptions of religious beliefs, rituals, practices, and discussions of their merits.

Why these constraints? When someone tells you what they believe, no matter how interested you are, it is natural for some level of disagreement or skepticism to arise, even subconsciously, which is a process of separation. Conversely, when someone shares their struggles and questions, it is natural for empathy to arise, which is a process of understanding and connection.

In putting this book together, we deliberately chose not to analyze the thousands of submissions we received with the intent of writing some profound conclusions (and presenting them as the only reasonable conclusions that could be derived), as that would violate the book's underlying premises.

In addition, as a photographer I have learned that when I explain a photograph to someone, in their mind it will always be mine (an expression of my experience); however, if I give them the opportunity to simply view the photograph, it can become theirs (their own emotional experience).

It is my desire that what you take from this book be born from your heart, and that you carry it with you as your own.

—Mark L. Tompkins

Student

Mark L. Tompkins, USA

INFLUENCE: CHRISTIANITY, SPIRITUALITY

Seed

Jennifer McMahon, USA

INFLUENCE: SPIRITUALITY

Piercing needle pulsing
sound primal drumbeat—
the depths of you

spirited hands whispering
hope divine passion—
echoes of you

sensual words seeking
womb sheltering warmth—
desire of you

urgent body impelling
fate fulfilling union—
origin of you

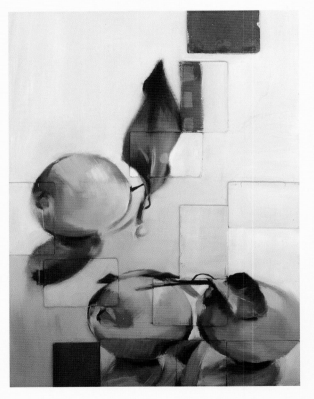

Three Lemons

Jill Hackney, USA

INFLUENCE: SPIRITUALITY

Introduction

Why compile a book of creative works based primarily on spiritual questions? Simply, it is precisely when we are struggling with doubts, confusion, misunderstandings, or the relentless, nagging sense that *there is something more*, that spiritual discovery begins:

> Why am I here? Is there a God? How can there be so much negativity and pain in the world? What is the purpose of life? Is there more to reality than what my five senses perceive, what I've been taught, what I've always believed to be true?

Psychologists tell us that the ego begins to develop around the age of two as a way of forming a sense of identity. No wonder then that the questions also begin at this age, the endless whys that allow the toddler to begin to make sense of the world and to explore the differences between you and me, self and other.

As we mature, the questions drive us, ideally, to a fuller understanding not only of who we are as individuals but also of our connection to the people and the world around us. They help us discover our roles in this lifetime and our relationship with God or spirit, nature, the universe. Whether we accept or reject the notion of a higher being, the underlying *question* must be considered as part of our self-exploration.

Illuminations sprang from the desire to examine the questions that are universal and timeless, then follow the questioning process as it leads along the spiritual journey, while simultaneously exploring disparate experiences, cultures, and spiritual beliefs.

By considering different perceptions and personal expressions of spirituality, we hope to gain enlightenment and a greater understanding of ourselves and others, while also celebrating the remarkable similarities that exist among truth seekers.

May this book provide moments of illumination for all who venture within.

—Jennifer McMahon

*"Be patient toward all that is unresolved in your heart
and try to love the questions themselves."*

—RAINER MARIA RILKE

How *Illuminations* Was Created

We received thousands of short stories, poems, photographs, and artworks from around the world in response to submission requests for pieces that express the personal spiritual experience, with special emphasis on:

- how beliefs are adopted or chosen
- dealing with questions and doubts
- determining how to live a spiritual life
- deciding if and how to worship
- connecting to one's spiritual nature
- moments of spiritual growth or disillusionment

In other words, pieces that explain either the *process* of spiritual exploration or the *spiritual person in action*, as opposed to ones that merely provide a statement of one's beliefs or practices.

Excerpted Poetry and Prose

In order to include as many viewpoints as possible and to conform to the book's theme, written pieces were often excerpted or edited. All excerpted pieces are noted in the List of Contributors (page 144); their full text can be found at www.IlluminationsBook.com/excerpts.

Spiritual Influences

In keeping with the personal nature of this collection, we included the spiritual or religious influence (expressing personal beliefs or creative inspiration) of contributors who chose to provide this information. In some cases both current and original (family/cultural) influences are noted.

Interviews

Scattered throughout the book are quotations or excerpts from interviews conducted either in person or online.

"The role of the artist I now understand as that of revealing through the world-surfaces the implicit forms of the soul . . ."

—JOSEPH CAMPBELL

Eclipse

Clare Walker, Wales

INFLUENCE: SPIRITUALITY

ASKING THE QUESTIONS
Uncertainties and Struggles that Lead to Spiritual Exploration

"Questions are the creative acts of intelligence."

—FRANK KINGDON

Eye of Hope—Series I

Lara Chauvin, Canada

INFLUENCE: ARMENIAN SPIRITUAL BELIEF, HOPE

October, Blue Cloud Abbey

Thom Tammaro, USA
INFLUENCE: ROMAN CATHOLICISM

In the chill of autumn, after vespers of cricket song and psalms sung by monks have quieted into the shadows of evening, long after the skies have darkened to indigo, we wrap ourselves in sweaters and walk the roads and bluffs around the abbey. A little wind sweeps the valley.

Our feet damp from the wet grass, we pause to watch someone pull the mist blanket over the valley and extinguish the last flickers of light at the edge of Minnesota. We talk in low voices, of galaxies, constellations, of distances, then gaze heavenward, amazed, to find the white arc and swirl of the Milky Way, Orion, and Polaris, always patient for us. We imagine distances we cannot understand and a place where no light reaches.

Who can be certain of the gravity of a life, the pull of the moment that gathers us, the way love draws one human heart to another? Three kings rode for twelve days across a desert following a star then offered gifts to Mary and the newborn child. The psalm tells us that darkness and light are both alike. But who tells us of the ache of living, or that love, like a star, is a light from another age just reaching us?

"I asked the elders about the creation of things and they told me it was God who created them; that is when I came up with the question of who created God or how did God come into existence."

—ADAMS MOSES, Nigeria
INFLUENCE: BAPTIST CHRISTIANITY

Dinner Roll Zen

Michael Meyerhofer, USA

INFLUENCE: ZEN BUDDHISM

(ORIGINAL: ROMAN CATHOLICISM)

Wandering into the kitchen,
he finds his wife pressing dough
to make dinner rolls. He pauses

in the sweet smell of the dough
and comments on how dinner rolls
which are, of course, the dough's

whole reason for being
cannot live up to this fine aroma,
as though something is always

lost in the act of becoming—
as though necessity breeds
the loss of some universal truth

to which his wife brushes flour
from her hands and tells him
to shut up and check the roast.

Birmingham Buddhist Centre, Rupa

Victor Burnside, England

INFLUENCE: BUDDHISM

Where Is God?

(TRANSLATED FROM THE ORIGINAL SPANISH
BY THE POET)

Nancy Bonsembiante, USA

Where is God
Who always hides?
It is not enough with faith
With vague ideas
With cheap sermons

I want to feel God
I want to touch him with my soul,
To feel him in the strangeness,
To cuddle him in the ridiculous,
To breathe him in the horror.

Sometimes my soul escapes,
My tears wear out,
My lips close,
My mind becomes consumed,
All empties in an unfair echo,
And I feel lonely.

Where is God
Who always hides?
If only your sight were enough
I'd build a lofty altar with your image
Where my soul could take refuge
When the nothingness surprises me.

His Presence

Reneé Dumont, USA

INFLUENCE: SEVENTH-DAY ADVENTIST CHURCH,
SABBATH KEEPER (ORIGINAL: BIBLE, SPIRITUAL
LEADERS)

On Meeting "Jesus"

C.C. Comber, England

INFLUENCE: SPIRITUAL JOURNEY FROM "NONBELIEVER"
TO "BELIEVER"

When we were kids,
there was this man we thought was
Jesus
'cause he looked like Jesus,
he had the sandals and everything,
that light, knowing smile,
a graciousness, those eyes;
yet rudely we'd gawp
as "He" padded silently past,
our chatter ebbing away
to nothing.

Years later (and purely by chance),
I was behind "Jesus" at the checkout
when I heard "Him" ask
for forty B&H and a bottle of Jack Daniels.

I was disappointed to say the least.

Prayer
Branislav Fabijanich, Croatia
INFLUENCE: CHRISTIANITY

*"Why was I only me, not also you? What made me, me?
Why was there all this tremendous suffering?*

*"I could not understand how I could be happy for even an instant
and yet know that somewhere, someone was being tortured, someone was
dying alone and in pain. This baffled me: how could I be so callous?
I saw that this was precisely why we can be so cruel. We have the capacity
to close ourselves off to others. If anything needed an answer, this did.
Where do I stop and you begin? What is the lie?"*

—EVA KIRCZ, Spain (birthplace: Holland)
INFLUENCE: HINDUISM, BUDDHISM, *A COURSE IN MIRACLES* (ORIGINAL: JUDAISM)

Marianne Williamson

USA, lecturer and author of *A Return to Love, Everyday Grace,* and others
INFLUENCE: JUDAISM, *A COURSE IN MIRACLES* (ORIGINAL: JUDAISM)

Was there a time when you questioned the nature of spirit and how to incorporate it into your life?

I think I have always wondered about God. I wondered about God as a child and I wonder about God now. For me, spiritual questioning is a lifelong process and the deeper our questioning, the deeper the answers when they are revealed.

Please describe your personal experience of those questions.

I think everybody has spiritual questions, it's just that most people do not know it. I do not see spiritual questions as divorced from any other questioning about the nature of reality and how we, as human beings, fit into it. I try not to see the spiritual quest as something precious, above or even separate from the quest to simply live a deeper and more meaningful life.

What led you in the direction of developing answers for yourself?

Being born. I think all of us are trying to find answers for ourselves. I don't think I am trying to find answers for myself any more than any other person. The act of breathing is immersion in God. Every moment is a challenge to live more fully who we really are. That is the spiritual path.

Why follow a spiritual path of any kind (as opposed to a particular path)?

I am a student of *A Course in Miracles*, not because the course tells me it is the only path, but simply because that's a path that spoke to me. The course is not a religion; it is psychological training in universal spiritual themes. Those universal spiritual themes are at the mystical core of all the great religious systems.

There is a story about a Buddhist monk pointing to the moon, and how some people mistakenly think the pointed finger is more important than the moon. The moon is what is important. Who points out the moon, which religion or spiritual path is pointing out the moon to us, is not the issue.

In *A Course in Miracles* it says that the world we live in is dominated by a thought system based on fear, and has been, literally, for ages. So if you simply allow your mind to be trained by the status quo thinking of the world, you get lost in a miasma of illusion and fear. The word *religion* comes from the Latin root *religio*, which means to bind back. True religion is a process of binding your mind back to truth while living in a world that lures you away from it. What path we walk to seek escape from the spiritual ignorance of the world is not the issue; the issue is that we come to realize the power of prayer, meditation, forgiveness, charity, and love in order to find the true light within us.

Do you identify primarily with one spiritual group, and is this the one you were introduced to as a child?

I am a Jew, and when you are born a Jew, you die a Jew. My Judaism informs my relationship to God very deeply, and it informs my philosophical, social, and political views of the world as well. Judaism calls us to repair the world, or *Tikun Olam*, as part of our mission, part of our responsibility to God and our community.

The Trip Through Solitude

Girish Kumar, India
INFLUENCE: CREATIVE SPIRITUAL ENERGY

The Flood

Swetha Raghunathan, India
INFLUENCE: HINDUISM

When the earth weeps
The wolf swims with sheep

Both question the heavens
Trying to find their brethren

Son of Kronos
Where are the heroes?

Created by chaos, from chaos,
Everything returns to chaos

God

Nancy Shiffrin, USA
INFLUENCE: JUDAISM

"If God can do anything how come
he let Goliath bother David in the first place?"

I arrange my food into armies,
meat against potatoes.
"Here's David and Goliath out front.
Where should I put Yawveh?
How come he's mad all the time?
How come there's no picture of him in my book?"

"At least finish your liver, then we'll talk about God."

"Why can't a girl be God?"

Synagogue Series #1

Kevin Katz, USA
INFLUENCE: REFORM JUDAISM (ORIGINAL: JUDAISM)

the stairs led
steeply downward
into
the vast
see
within me

that had yet to be
discovered.

Vast See
Michele Renée Ledoux, USA
INFLUENCE: EXTRAORDINARINESS OF THE ORDINARY

9

A Struggle for Faith and Freedom

Z. Foo, South Africa

INFLUENCE: ISLAM

How do we know that what we know *is* true? For me this question is a lifelong search. I was born and raised Muslim in South Africa during apartheid. The government determined what we would believe, what our values would be, how we would live, what questions to ask, and what answers to receive.

My soul yearned for freedom, longed to feel its essence. If you had asked me what a Muslim was, I would have answered that it is one who prays, gives alms, believes in one god, and fasts. But a religion cannot be classified according to its constitution nor a believer identified through her practices. Faith for me is about what the heart feels, not what the mind says or the body does. So the suffocating restrictions of the state made me long for an inner freedom, a more loving authority, a just way of life, and a peace that transcends human limitations.

Is this world capable of giving peace? How can love and comfort be found in nature or human relationships that are finite? Or is it possible only in another world, a spiritual world that transcends time, space, and earthly restrictions? Can peace be attained only when one has a connection to a higher being? Is prayer the means of achieving this communion? Connection with god is when I feel god's presence in everything I do, when I know that he is with me, watching me every minute of every day. Peace with god, for me, is when I please him, worship him, obey his commandments, and live for him, because it is due to him that I am alive.

It is not an easy process, nor is it complete. Every moment we make decisions that either take us closer to god or farther from him.

Day Dream
Mehdi S. Sabet, United Arab Emirates
INFLUENCE: ISLAM

Identity Struggle

Margarita Gokun Silver, USA (birthplace: USSR [Russia])
INFLUENCE: JUDAISM

"Actually, I'm not really Russian."

When I lived in Russia it was still part of the Soviet Union. My passport had a line listing my *natsionalnost*, or ethnic origin. We, the Jews, called this line *pyatii punkt*, the fifth line, and knew that it was the most important piece of information our passports contained. Every Soviet citizen had that line—Ukrainians were written as Ukrainian, Uzbeks as Uzbek—but it was only for Jews that it mattered. For whenever people mentioned those fateful words, they spoke of the discrimination that only Jews can experience.

Pyatii punkt were the words people whispered when they explained why someone didn't get the job, promotion, or visa to travel abroad. In short, the fifth line was there to remind us that we indeed *were not* Russian and never would be.

(continued)

As a small child, insulted by classmates and sometimes picked on by teachers, I desperately wanted to fit in. I despised being Jewish, hated the idea of not being Russian, and only wanted to belong, be part of the crowd. As a teenager, I concealed my *pyatii punkt* hoping not to be noticed, yet no longer hated being a Jew. Somewhere between childhood and adolescence I learned that my Jewishness wasn't something to be ashamed of. I learned that I belong to a community of people who, although often detested, are always strong and united. I learned that I belong to a nation, wherever in the world it may be. And I came to terms with the fact that I'll never belong to the country where I was born and raised.

I left the Soviet Union fleeing anti-Semitism and religious persecution. I knew nothing about my religion, except that I wanted to remain Jewish and celebrate it in the open. But I didn't know how. Having grown up in a society where religion was branded "the opiate of the people," my knowledge of Judaism was limited to an occasional Yom Kippur fast or a rare Rosh Hashanah celebration. I had to start from the very beginning.

That start was almost fifteen years ago and I am still learning, including how to let go of the old skepticism of everything religious, to believe, and to have faith. It's not easy or comfortable, but it will bring me closer to where I want to be.

The God I Know

Sibusisiwe Nkomo, USA (birthplace: Zimbabwe)
INFLUENCE: SKEPTICISM (ORIGINAL: CHRISTIANITY)

I have always been aware that I would someday have to choose between my desires and my spiritual beliefs. My life is a constant struggle to marry the two.

"Why am I here? What is the purpose of my life? Why is it so hard to remember that being connected to the source of all is why I am?"

—SITA D'OYEN, USA

The Murderer on Her Cot

K.B. Hollingsworth, USA

INFLUENCE: NATURE, SURREALISM, EXISTENTIALISM (ORIGINAL: CHRISTIANITY, EST, OTHERS)

A moment in nothing
but moments. another loose thread.
it is raveled
and added
to the pile.

the skull-shaved lama says
i am a light in a string of lights
lit from one flame leaping
from wick to wick.
once i was a blue-skinned deity
with flesh of oak
and scores of limbs
dancing on the heads of water,
the heads of fire.
once a saint who ate
her own eyes for breakfast.
now this.
loosened and muting,
i've passed from resolution
to dissolution;
a secondary state
akin to fluid. and in moments
the sizzle rattle will shoot me
into the density of zephyrs
and shades.

instead,
i think of heaven
the old paradise of Sunday school
cotton sheep roaming crayoned fields
and chinks of dawn through a cloudbank
was all that represented ascendance,
before the sun was only one star
in a scattering of stars.
how tightly i could almost see it
my eyes compressed
and i was certain.

we should be
we should be allowed to visit
as shades
as zephyrs
while we still have breath

a moment in nothing
but moments. another loose thread.
it is raveled
and added
to the pile.

"Why do bad things happen all the time? If someone could control my life and this place, then do they hate me?"

—KELLY WEBB, Australia (birthplace: England)
INFLUENCE: ATHEISM (ORIGINAL: PROTESTANT CHRISTIANITY)

Philosopher

Ruth Calder Murphy, England

Thanks, Descartes.
Already, I am dizzy,
reeling from the edge of implications.
I am, therefore I think.
Or is it the other way round after all?
Maybe a mind greater than mine is thinking me into being,
toying with my complexities only to blink me to oblivion.
Perhaps I am an idea in the mind of God.
Is God's mind so great that such an idea—
Ego, I—
is an amazing thing?
Perhaps I am treasured,
an idea in a million,
or insignificant as a drop in the ocean.
I think, therefore I am,
but what am I?

The Tower of Ego

Oleg Korolev, Ukraine (birthplace: Russia)

INFLUENCE: ORTHODOX CHRISTIANITY,

HESYCHASM (ORIGINAL: ART)

God's Closet

Susan Rich, USA

"Your capabilities are as wide as God's closet"
        —August Wilson

So is God a clotheshorse, wild for the end-of-season sales?
How many pairs of sandals can a deity wear at one time?
Open-toed canvas? Sturdy soles and stilettos?

Is her closet an attic wardrobe piled high with garden gnomes?
Does she hide her love letters there, a cat's eye, tins of silver foil?
The Koran? The Bible? Does she sometimes hide herself?

Perhaps it's a cedar closet full of muted colors, one fox stole?
Would she wear leather gloves, a seal-skin coat?
Why keep a closet for things at all? Candlelit dinners? The Mardi Gras Ball?

Then is God a materialist? Must she dress for success?
Who does she dine with on Fridays? Moses and Mohamed?
Is God good company? The life of the party or utterly serious?

Is hers a memory vault of skeletons—plagues, fires, and floods?
Or replete with miracles, manna washed in honeyed light?
Is this where God goes to sleep? Who calls to whisper good night?

When God gets lonely, does she play the fool? Could her heart break?
Her closet extend enough for two? Does she yearn for a daughter?
What next is a God with a closet going to do?

"Who am I? What is the spirit, and how do I develop a direct experience of it?
And is there a clear method that becomes objective yet personal?
. . . A question becomes a quest, and every answer
becomes the next question leading further along the path."

—IAIN B. TROUSDELL, New Zealand (birthplace: England)
INFLUENCE: DIRECT EXPERIENCE OF SPIRIT (ORIGINAL: NONDENOMINATIONAL CHRISTIANITY)

A Memo to God

Carol Smallwood, USA
INFLUENCE: QUESTIONING GOD

Hello God:

It sounds disrespectful, but how else can I address You? Dear God doesn't sound right and Our Father Who Art in Heaven sounds too remote.

The reason evil occurs is that man ate from the Tree of Knowledge given to him by a woman—but if You're all-knowing, You knew it would happen.

And God, as a woman, I feel a special anger. Why was I made from Adam's rib as an afterthought to make him happy—doesn't that reflect a lack of planning? What chance did I have, physically weaker in a world where the strongest survive? Women are the ones to have children (and why use such a painful way?), and once we're raised, we aren't needed. Why did you make Your mother a virgin? And, couldn't You've arranged that monthly thing differently?

I don't think I'd call You a gentleman: You've set us in the middle of an expressway, and yet we're to give You praise each day we aren't smashed. I don't mind being smashed, but it's lingering half-alive that's inexcusable. Why didn't You make the earth more hospitable before making life?

In some Eastern religions, deity and soul are one, but in Christianity, God and soul are separate. I think the Eastern way's better because if You made man in Your image, the Ten Commandments wouldn't have been necessary. The old Catholic Church may have been the smartest of all: it told man he was sinful, and guilt helped build unprecedented cathedrals and masterpieces.

Still, if I don't believe You exist, why do I yearn that You do? You are Divine, I'm human; I have as much chance knowing You as an ant walking to the moon. Caroline said that You were love, and I think she believes it. I think if You ever appear, I'll be cutting my toenails because You like absurdity.

Homeless

Judy Halebsky, USA

INFLUENCE: WRITING POETRY

Me, I'm kind of like a go-cart
thrown together and tied on
hoping to hold up through the end of the course
to stop flooding the engine
throw away all the regrets and complaints
to laugh at all the good parts
I'm trying to soften my heart

the work isn't easy
I have to believe that this life is some kind of miracle
that everyone struggles, even the rich college kids
that there's beauty here in the taqueria's bright yellow paint, the empty car lot,
liquor stores and drive-ins, the teenage girls with new jeans and hairspray

that I can do
but how to see Otis washing windows at the street light as different from me
how to see the dragged-out poor kids as part of the landscape
I think that might take more than I've got
or at least more than I want to have

"Why was I born? There must be a specific reason for it.
I should be useful to others provided I am not abused or exploited."

—SRIJAYA CHAR, India

Cover Me

Wilma Kenny, Northern Ireland

INFLUENCE: CHRISTIANITY

Cover me in autumn leaves
falling
falling
nature's reward.

Compensation
for their strife and greed
which fell sharp and sore
taking my sight.

I now stride among
those who pushandshove
like falling
shrapnel from high towers
searching for You
among the debris.

Sketch

Marcus Antonius Jansen, USA

INFLUENCE: SPIRITUALITY

Crying Out Loud In Jerusalem

Bonnie Nish, Canada

INFLUENCE: SEEKING (ORIGINAL: JUDAISM)

The birds fly south
it is too soon to give up
this burning bush
and fly with them.
I chop onions to cry
in the middle of the night
the staccato of my knife
pierces the silence
and I feel less alone.
What are the words for home?
When you lose the flock
there is no one left to translate.

The breaking of an hourglass
stuns me into movement,
trying to put the world
back together bit by bit,
tripping over glass
the mind escapes this desert of pain
to nest at the foot of the Wailing Wall.
There are broken wings piled here
I cannot touch them
but understand how loose feathers
can bring you peace.

Dust and Sin

Gopal Lahiri, India

Flowing river
Steady currents
Ripples go by.

Shed my clothes
Slip into water
Shivering cold.

Should I swim?
Should I sink?
Wash my dust and sin.

I must find
A shelter of peace
Farther than this life.

Semones

Catherine Seitz Funk, USA

INFLUENCE: PAGANISM

They asked about you
after the funeral
there was nothing I could say, so
I slipped away when it grew so hot
I knew no one would follow
down through the fault and up and over
to the trail, past the ghost of the carnation house
no longer brave enough to go barefoot
over smoke trees without you
not wanting to be a stranger
in another family's grief

One last visit to the grove
to swim in the clear cold shallows
alone after too many years dreaming
from too far away

The trail ends in brush where a path should be
I climbed through the prickly red weeds
wishing for my forgotten
boots and Levi's
protection from the gouging branches

I came out in a clearing to find that
someone dropped a cement bench
in the middle of my memory
it was covered in bird shit
and looking ashamed

The creosote was trying to hide it—
a convenience for any tourists
who might be afraid of dirt
I stood on top of the thing to find
the pond filled in with
cattails and duckweed
once grassy banks grown tall and thick
now made impassable by sludge

Only the regal palms remain unchanged
untouched by time
standing proud in their
shaggy golden robes
forming the eternal shadow circle
forever silent
and cool as a final kiss

I am humbled at their feet
watching the ants go about their business
finding food in the pebbles
water in the sand
I pave trails with my fingers
and change their world forever

A breeze of slight green shadows
whispers of wisdom
far above my head
out of reach

I lie on top of the alien bench to claim this thing
that I am not strong enough to move
some truce must be made here
a peace exchanged
I pray to gods who
no longer remember my name

The mosquitoes come
to tell me that
the tiny silver fish have left the lake,
the floods will come again
to take this all and no one will remember
what came before

My anger startles the dirt gray lizards
moving slow enough to be
easily caught
I would wish for a hawk blessing
but I think she has not chosen me today

The cement grows hard against my back
a canyon of stillness
deep as a martyr's last thought
creeps through the moss and yellowed reeds
and steals the air from the wind
with stunning silence

Magic is still stalking in this grove
it is in this cool soft dust
blown that I have bathed in
from the decaying palm fronds
heaped in piles on the sand
the spiders spin it into the creosote,
the bite of desert green,
as they have since I have known them
or for a thousand years, forgotten

Tecolote
I am waiting for a sign, but
I know that you are sleeping
high in the treetops hiding safe until
the moon staggers above the bluffs

The wonder remains
and will grow
a thousand times greater than when
the old man with warm desert-worn hands
walked with us
to watch it grow and feed it

The dunes seem to have slid closer
grown smaller
still keeping their secrets
treasures to be hidden from
the tenderfeet, who never carry
enough water to get past them
I grow warm in the burning sun
and cold in the shade

He would tell me to put a pebble
in my mouth to quench my thirst
take my hand and show me
something I had overlooked
in the cathedral

The palms lanky green fingertips
encircle a patch of blue sky above
their language tastes like raindrops
and wisdom splashing in the sand
while I walk away evading

Everything that is beautiful and
everyone who is not here
the dead and the lost, what was
what I thought would be

I take the wrong trail and trap myself
in the brush, disgusted
a twig snaps
I turn to see a coyote shadow
following me, smiling he
leads me through the brush
back to the path, keeping casual company

Hoping to be remembered for
more than his wicked irony

"Is there a hand (fate) that influences us, sometimes in a way undesirable? Would we be able to please It (or Him or Her or Xi [any other sex])?"

—OLUBUNMI GABRIEL OSHO-DAVIES, China (birthplace: Nigeria)
INFLUENCE: PENTECOSTAL CHRISTIANITY (ORIGINAL: TRADITIONAL BELIEFS)

Requiring God

Elizabeth Heaney, USA
INFLUENCE: AVATAR MEHER BABA (ORIGINAL: ROMAN CATHOLICISM)

At first, it just seemed like a normal "bump in the road" on a spiritual path: a little more challenge connecting with God? No worries. I would just be patient and the connection would resurface before long. Only it didn't. In fact, as the months went by, the sense of disconnection became absolute. I reached out to God in any way I could imagine. I went to therapists. I sought out priests and ministers. I visited communes and spiritual groups. I prayed—and then prayed harder. I stood in my backyard and screamed at the sky for help and comfort. I curled into a ball in my room and felt more alone than I could have ever imagined . . . and still I called out to God. But nothing touched the yawning gap inside of me. . . .

"I want two things," I said. "I want to feel my heart again. And I want to know I have a relationship with God—a tangible, palpable relationship. I can't have it based on faith anymore. I ran out of faith a long time ago."

Untitled

Attila Futaki, Hungary

2
FOLLOWING A PATH
Seeking Answers by Embracing
a Belief System

*"True freedom lies in the realization and calm acceptance of
the fact that there may well be no perfect answer."*

—ALLEN REID MCGINNIS

Imprints

Wenceslas Chevalier, France
INFLUENCE: FRAGILITY OF HUMAN BEING
(ORIGINAL: LOVE OF HUMANITY)

The Way They Departed

Kamau Rucker, USA

INFLUENCE: UNDECIDED, CHRISTIANITY (ORIGINAL: BAPTIST/EVANGELICAL CHRISTIANITY)

He didn't stand like the others.
His posture was not stooped.
His eyes didn't have a far-off look.
There was a fire in his speech.
He was not a prisoner.
He listened to every word
And reminded you to breathe.
He spoke to you of eternity.

For you, he was the source,
He was the way,
He was release,
He was raw truth,
He was transformation,
He was all ears
Giving you affirmation.
You realized the whole of it that night.

You ran back in song,
Ran back in silence,
Ran back bowing and begging,
Ran back proselytizing,
Ran back with wings,
Ran back with quills,
Crying out and dancing
Heavy with the burden of gifts;

Into the ether,
Taking seven steps,
Eyes turned up,
Spouting words like a gunboat,
Sailing through the air,
To the four corners,
Still,
For eternity.

Krishna, Buddha, Jesus,
Allah, MLK, the apostles,
Gandhi, the ancestors, roads.

Rainbow Turban

Gautam Narang, United Kingdom

Temple Reflections in the Ganges

ShantiMayi, France

INFLUENCE: INDIGENOUS WISDOM, EASTERN RELIGION, CHRISTIANITY

(ORIGINAL: RUSSIAN ORTHODOX CHURCH)

This Mountain My Life

Lauren Crux, USA

INFLUENCE: SPIRITUAL QUESTIONING, IRONY

Brilliant white, braced
against cobalt blue,
Manaslu Himal,
Manasulu,
the Sherpas call it.

I stood on the pass
not needing to climb its jagged peak.
I listened for a voice,
hoped for a burning bush.

I thought the mountain's hugeness
would humble me,
that I might rediscover my
insignificance,
but in awe,
all purpose fell away.

The mountain did not speak,
it breathed, through me.
Again and again, until there was
no I, until there was no mountain.
This is where God was born.
I am not a believer
there was simply no doubt.

I did not return mist-eyed, nor
mystic. I am not gentled,
the mountains are not gentle.

Enlightenment is momentary,
the master said, *all the rest
is remembrance and practice.*

Birdy

Ronya Shvachka, Israel
(birthplace: Ukraine)
INFLUENCE: MY SON
(ORIGINAL: CHRISTIANITY)

A Bird on a Wire

Judy Halebsky, USA
INFLUENCE: WRITING POETRY

At Big Al's Paradise the girls are singing for free the preachers are adding more chairs

the only thing I made it through was high school drunk driving jumping off cliffs into rivers hitching
     rides and that groping boy with stubby claw hands

   the true story is   there's a slow hum   a gray falling

and maybe every person is trying for some kind of escape
some guarantee of safety   some kind of freedom

             and the promise to die going straight to heaven or having
nothing hidden within their soul   or loving with such intensity that it's bigger than this
moment   than our small lives   than our broken bone bodies

         surviving doesn't really have the same appeal when you hold it up to the
other options say salvation or being a hero or maybe even becoming unbreakable

Somnambulists

Dmytro Drozdovsky, Ukraine

I dreamed my breastbone
parted in the darkness,
spilling a dim stream
of roses, lilies,
chalices for bees,
my heart became a hive
of wings, a chamber
graven with your name,
magnified by droning
of monastic choirs
in miniature,

each syllable expanding
into eulogies and dithyrambs,
distilled and metamorphosed
into honey of pure praise.

I dreamed my skin
exuded myrrh
and frankincense,
and recognizing
you, the tree of life
inside me bloomed again,
birds fluttered
from between my ribs
as if the cage could not
contain them,
as you raised your hands
like a somnambulist
to touch my face.

Simplicity

Prudence Page, USA

INFLUENCE: BREATH, EXPLORATION . . .

I want to go to a monastery
where simplicity sits on the wood floor
the great monolith of noise
quivers and is gone

and there is only one to conquer
the same of many sly faces
but the same one

the walls of the monastery
remind me moment by moment
why I am here
each footstep echoes
"listen"
and whispers on

and perhaps the master will snap her fingers
and say
"there!"
and I will see it
the bridge
from one infinity to the next
inside eternity
and beyond

yes, beyond
I have been there
and snapped back—a stone
in a sling
not yet released

A Question of Calling

Dharmachari Maitreyabandhu, England

INFLUENCE: BUDDHISM

I misread it. Craning to see Caravaggio's massive canvas, *The Calling of St. Matthew*, I thought Christ's call had not yet been heard; that Levi the tax collector was pointing at the handsome, sullen youth counting his money at the end of the table. Completely absorbed in their world of finance, neither he nor the older man behind, adjusting his spectacles, has noticed the visitors. Christ is almost hidden behind his barefoot escort (probably St. Peter), his raised hand—calling—and thin line halo barely visible. He *summons*, "Follow me," his feet already turning to leave.

But I misread it, thinking this particular religious conversion still in progress, the call winging its way to the man at the end of the table, the moment *before* the dawning of knowledge.

Calling . . . I had never thought of it like that. I had always been aware that the *reasons* I gave for being a Buddhist were post-hoc rationalizations of dubious veracity. I knew I was a Buddhist, but could not say *why* . . . or if I could, was never totally convinced myself, as if my real motivation was too deep to reason or explain (or at least *finish* explaining).

Buddhists don't talk in terms of being "called." The impulse to practice Buddhism seems simpler—a straightforward response to the human situation. On the face of it there's nothing *mystical* about Buddhism . . . it's enlightened common sense.

And for Buddhists there's no one to do the calling anyway: no God to shine His celestial light down. So why did this painting affect me so deeply? Why the giddying uplift, the heart-clamor? At first, all I knew was that something resonated deep within me, as if the painting were saying "You *know* me . . . you know me very well." Christ's "follow me" is a demand. Someone must obey. Christ's hidden body emphasizes the force of his calling, concentrating our attention on his shadowed, mysterious face and raised, emblematic hand. The light coursing down from above seems to be a part of him, as if it were *his* vision searching this dark space for an answering light.

Looking at it, I started to wonder if I was having a religious conversion myself. But gradually I felt my way through the intricacies of my response—the light, the closed room, Christ's summons, and the youth slouching at the end of the table. Something

The Calling of Saint Matthew

Caravaggio

1599–1600, CONTARELLI CHAPEL, SAN LUIGI DIE FRANCESI, ROME

about this young man: a self-absorbed, what's-the-point attitude that I recognized from my own life.

Caravaggio's painting dramatizes my own sense of spiritual life, my struggles and moments of realization. The boy in my misreading does not know he has been called: head down, focused on worldly things, unaware of the light and the light-bringer. Yet into this closed world, Christ appears; from outside, beyond "me" and "mine." He brings illumination.

It reminds me, darkly, how I felt when I was young and largely preoccupied with mundane things, counting my pennies. If I got what I wanted, I felt happy for a time—though in a self-intoxicated way. If I didn't, or if I got what I did *not* want, I was moody and bad-tempered. I was often bored, unsatisfied. But something seemed to call me, to whisper dissatisfactions in my ear.

Then one day, after putting it off for weeks, I rushed across London to the Buddhist Center. I only had a moment to be amused by the large golden Buddha dominating the room (though it also strangely elated me). That evening we tried to focus on our breathing. . . . I think I nodded off.

Halfway through the introduction to meditation, which was not especially inspiring, I realized that I was a Buddhist. It was not a strong experience, more akin to the simple recognition of a fact—like finding out the name of a tree I had long been familiar with. "Oh *that's* what I am."

Like Levi in Caravaggio's painting, I had seen the light. For he is not pointing to his sulky neighbor. He is pointing to himself. He seems tense and about to stand, as if drawn inexorably to Christ. Levi is caught between the world and the Light, one hand frozen in the moment of laying down a small silver coin, the other pointing, amazed, at himself. "You mean *me*?"

It took a while to sort all this out, the strength of my first reading resonating so strongly with my past that it was some time before I realized my mistake. But if my first misreading reminded me of my life *before* I became a Buddhist, my second "correct" interpretation resonated with my experience of *becoming* a Buddhist—and with my life ever since.

Christ's divine interruption decisively changed Levi/Matthew's life. Perhaps for St. Matthew it was straightforward (if not exactly easy). He followed his Lord without looking back, without wandering off or losing faith. The moment of his calling was *the* moment—a complete change of heart, a turning away from the world and a turning toward God.

It has not been like that for me. *Mine* was a change in direction, in orientation. Becoming a Buddhist, more than anything else, gave me a sense of purpose, a goal, and a path. I knew it would not be easy. For spiritual illumination to change us completely, the light must penetrate down to the bottom of our hearts, with nothing left over. For most of us it is never quite like that.

My life certainly changed. I imagined myself like some devout monk, smiling blissfully into the void while vacuuming. But I was not saved. I could still be moody, resentful (albeit in that polite English way), and unhappy . . . in fact for a while things seemed to get worse. If indeed I *was* following my Lord Buddha, I kept getting lost, looking back, grumbling about the difficulty of the journey, and taking cigarette breaks. I was not St. Matthew.

I had been called nonetheless. Enough light had entered my heart to change me irrevocably, but not enough to change me *completely*. Imagine Caravaggio's painting as a series of short films. In one, St. Matthew follows his Lord; in the next he does not look up from his money counting, he refuses, *resists*. In the next he follows but only partway; then he doubts, disbelieves, follows again. Next he is made to feel a fool; then thinks he is one. It has been like that for me.

The calling has sometimes been sweet: a soft, gentle voice urging me on; sometimes sharp: a hard, insistent dog-bark in the backyard. If I wander too far from spiritual life, the barking starts up again. Nowadays, I think of my life in terms of a gradual, increasing willingness to cooperate with some deep and hidden force (within me or outside of me?). The struggle is to give in.

But I had never thought of it as being "called," not until that day in front of Caravaggio's work. And it was not a *thought* exactly, more a realization, like being shown an underlying reality that I had forgotten or mislaid. I had been summoned. I *would* follow . . . I could not help myself.

"Each one of us is pure and therefore it is our responsibility to clean the dust on our way and walk ahead toward our destinies. Following a spiritual path and feeling the divine touch is leading toward destiny in its own way."

—DEEPA, India

Reflections on Spirituality

Charlene T. Pollano, USA

INFLUENCE: BOOKS ON SPIRITUALITY (ORIGINAL: ROMAN CATHOLICISM)

It is what I don't understand and what I'm not comfortable with that drives my spiritual journey. Life has its shimmering moments when the world glistens with contentment, even joy. I have these moments, and that's perhaps when I'm lazy about my spirituality, since I'm comfortable.

My spirituality is fleeting, like the leaves I see skittering across the lawn. I need it to be more grounded—solid—available to me at all times. Uppermost in my soul, at least. This is what I strive for through my writing.

I love what Anne Lamott said in *Traveling Mercies.* She talks about her path of spirituality as happening in "fits and starts." Mine is more like stepping on land mines every few years! Blowing myself up, falling down to earth in pieces, regrouping and searching, then accepting that there is a purpose. I need to learn about land mine detection. Or—how to fly!

Clouds

Ismael Covarrubias, USA

INFLUENCE: BUDDHIST CHANT *NAM-MYO-HO-REN-GE-KYO*

"It is very important to follow the path of my religion, because this is the only right path that our true messenger showed us. If we do what our God wants, we will get everything we want."

—SHERAZ, Pakistan
INFLUENCE: ISLAM

"I now believe there is only one path to God. I know it is a bitter truth, but it must be told and in love."

—ABD AL-SOBUR, Nigeria
INFLUENCE: CHRISTIANITY (ORIGINAL: ISLAM)

"Spirituality is our own expression within ourselves of 'who I am' and of belonging within our communities; it is also the bread in our lives and souls. Spirituality is important, but depends upon each person to internalize their faith and beliefs. But there is freedom of choice for everyone."

—SOPHIA RUFINO DIMALOG, Philippines
INFLUENCE: ISLAM

"As Augustine of Hippo said: **My heart is restless until it rests in You.** *Yet, as I have realized, resting in God actually demands a genuine commitment to God and to my neighbor. It is not an escape from life but exactly the opposite. Resting in God, as I see it, is only the beginning of a life of commitment and responsibility.*

—RUBEN C. MENDOZA, Belgium (birthplace: Philippines)
INFLUENCE: ROMAN CATHOLICISM

"

Heinz Gods (57 varieties)

John Irvine, New Zealand

INFLUENCE: SPIRITUAL VIEW OF LIFE (ORIGINAL: SPORADIC RELIGIOUS AFFILIATION)

Tonight
as I wove
a wobbly path
home from the local shop
just a bit pissed
with Diet Coke
for my budget rum
I wondered about god.

It's rather interesting
thinking about god.

In the shop I went to
the man wore his
dark, uncut hair
twirled up in a knot,
and bound with cloth.
Apparently his god
liked it that way
and felt it a requirement
for entry into that
particular heaven.
His beard was also a-twirl
under his chin
uncut.
Hirsuteness
is a requirement
for Sikh Heaven
I guess.

Walking home
I saw a blind man
striding purposefully along,
looking at his
personal world from within
white stick weaving a pattern
only he comprehends.
Does his god
require him to be blind
to find heaven?
Do you think?

Then there was
a small, chubby woman
in a colorful oriental garment.
She had her head
and body completely covered—
her god apparently
doesn't like flesh.
Even her eyes
were unavailable for comment.
A curious god indeed.

I have a very dear friend
who is young and vital
and dying.
I suppose her god
requires the suffering
for her to become
heavenly.

My folks love god
they are gentle people
loving and caring
yet their god is vengeful . . .
their symbols
are Fire and Blood.
Now that's scary . . .

If I were a Buddhist monk
I would need to wear saffron
and not step on ants.
Do you think gods
have a thing about colors?
Or ants?

As for me . . . well, I don't know.
I think I lost my god a while ago
whoever he may have been.
Or she.

Being drunk helps . . .
I don't have to think
about it much then
or wonder about
all the different ways
we think we need
to be special
in heavenly terms.

I think I'll just stay drunk.
The world seems
better more often,
and for a lot longer that way.

Gods are just too confusing . . .

Neil, Roy, and the Spirit

John Sumner, USA

"I really believe that religion divides and spirituality unites. People are at all different stages of enfoldment and enlightenment (or lack of). Basically people need a compass, a remembrance of who we are and what it feels like to be in spirit."

—REV. HOWARD E. CAESAR, USA

INFLUENCE: UNITY, UNIVERSAL SPIRITUAL TEACHINGS (ORIGINAL: LUTHERAN CHURCH)

"I feel that following a spiritual path is dictated by society. We have been told that only blind faith or inner peace will help us survive this harsh world. We've been taught to fear an alternative worse than . . . (insert your biggest fear, death, for example).

"I was living in a puritan world where I believed my carnal desires were wrong, my African heritage obsolete. Where my desires, ambitions, religion, and soul were at war with each other. I needed to find peace, with or without god."

—SIBUSISIWE NKOMO, USA (birthplace: Zimbabwe)
INFLUENCE: SKEPTICISM (ORIGINAL: CHRISTIANITY, TRADITIONAL AFRICAN BELIEFS)

Shifting Sand

Hank Binnema, Canada (birthplace: The Netherlands)
INFLUENCE: EARTH SPIRITUALITIES, UNITARIANISM (ORIGINAL: CHRISTIAN REFORMED CHURCH, DUTCH CALVINISM)

The sliding bar moves ceaselessly
Shifting sand, shifting sand
Weight of the spheres of rhetoric
Propelling us downward into our masks.

The mask soldered to my face
Shifting sand, shifting sand
Snuffs out the candle of my heart
My body weighted forward to fill the gap.

My stomach is in constant motion
Shifting sand, shifting sand
Agitated by the poisonous codes
Kept in to protect the fragile mask.

I crave a fortress of perfection and transparent
   truth
Shifting sand, shifting sand
Tall castellated cliffs give way to
Loose mounds of ice-sculptured fossils.

Shifting sand, shifting sand
Freedom to move, freedom to slide down
Freedom to create codes, and smash them.
Shifting sand, shifting sand.

A Symphony of One

David McGoy, USA

INFLUENCE: NATURE, THE UNIVERSE (ORIGINAL: PENTECOSTAL CHRISTIANITY, JEHOVAH'S WITNESSES)

If only the stone could hear
the symphony that plays in his ears
but stone is stone.

swinging with rhythm blues and soul
the symphony plays the stone just hovers and
    hums
worlds to come deeds undone.

with open horn and closed eyes
the determined player tries to keep
the slumbering stone from falling
out of step.

the rhythms take you for a ride
but there's no steady beat to guide
to keep the time the way time
was meant to be kept.

set sail across waters of success
his blues now echo in a bay of disinterest
his soul adrift in a harbor
of emptiness

weighted down by unkept time
fooled by orchestral maneuvers of the mind
the player plays with pride as his dream
silently dies.

as every lonely note
drowns in an indifferent sea of stone.

so in solitude he hears his muted melody
subtle harmonies beneath humming deeds
    undone
devoted to a philharmonic fancy
the player plays a symphony of one.

Artist & Muse

David Dalessandro, USA

I Stood Once at the Edge of It

Jennifer Morrow, Canada
INFLUENCE: EKNATH EASWARAN AND PASSAGE MEDITATION (ORIGINAL: ANGLICANISM)

I stood once at the edge of it—
did not leap, for fear of it.

Running down this darkened hall,
a life spent without thought of it.

A humble man gave me a book.
I winced against the light of it.

In the hallway there's a door.
Slow down, feel for the shape of it.

The leaves were torn, a hollow made.
A key lay hid in the pages of it.

Smooth panels and—yes—a rusty knob—
and light glowed dim from the base of it.

The key did fit, though the door is stiff—
but with your grace I'll open it.

"Finding answers to my questions is a matter of freedom to me. Who in me is running the show? Why do I make the decisions I do, and what is the process in this? Hopefully I can find some deeper integrity and let it grow, and help me (whoever me is!) do the right things, for those around me and my life course."

—IAIN B. TROUSDELL, New Zealand (birthplace: England)
INFLUENCE: DIRECT EXPERIENCE OF SPIRIT (ORIGINAL: NONDENOMINATIONAL CHRISTIANITY)

"In following a 'spiritual path,' I no longer had to depend solely on myself; I was able to trust without doubt that something else was at play in my life besides what I could think of on a conscious level. Over time, I realized I was correct. Something on an unconscious level had always been telling me that if I could identify my own spirituality, I would no longer have to depend entirely on left-brained, linear thinking."

—TOBIAS BEHARRELL, Canada
INFLUENCE: TRUST IN A GREATER PLAN / POWER (ORIGINAL: LITTLE TO NONE)

Fire (That Does Not Burn)

T. Geronimo Johnson, USA

INFLUENCE: TIBETAN BUDDHISM, CATHOLICISM, J. KRISHNAMURTI
(ORIGINAL: CATHOLICISM, CHARISMATIC CHRISTIANITY)

This fire has no beginning
this fire speaks of spirits that always were
   and never will not be
this fire is silent wind, eternal
   in source-less light
this fire is the splendor
   of a thousand suns
and the shadow of
   a thousand moons
this fire is Krishna
   Vishnu, Brahmin
this fire is Ganesh gone wild
this fire heals, cauterizes, blinds
   this fire salves
   the civil rights suture that bind
   a thousand black Americans
   (and all survivors of all holocausts
   and all passengers of the middle passage
   called earth)
   into a teaming mass of glorious wounds
   from which flowers now grow
this fire is Christ
this fire is Buddha
this fire is Boddhisattva
   Yahweh
   Allah
this fire is the chill
   in your spine

and the disembodied voice
   that wrestles your consciousness
   and tills your soul
   till it doth bleed
   to bear new fruit
this fire tolerates no maya
this fire frees the demons
   and then consumes them
this fire everyone knows
for this fire rests
humbly, patiently, awaiting discovery
in all of our souls

Doorscape 23

David Vincent Hammer, Australia
INFLUENCE: SPIRITUALITY, CHRISTIANITY

Holy Ghost at Heart Lake

Helen Ruggieri, USA

INFLUENCE: BUDDHISM, QUAKERISM (ORIGINAL: PRESBYTERIANISM)

Heart Lake was owned by an evangelical, Pentecostal group, and our church rented it at least twice a year for "outings." It was not good swimming. As you approached the water you could hear the kerplunk of frogs and (I was sure) deadly water snakes that wrapped around you and pulled you to the bottom of the lake where you'd disappear in the muck and your body would never be found.

I always wanted to scoop up a handful of water and make the sign of the cross on my chest like some kids did at the beach. *It's so Mary won't let us drown*, some kid had told me. I liked that. I never quite had the nerve though. Especially not at Heart Lake.

I loved to swim, cutting the water with that crisp overhand stroke I'd picked up watching Esther Williams in the movies. So it was difficult to pass up an opportunity, even if you had to wade out through disgusting muck that slimed up over the tops of your feet. I'd brave the muck for a swim.

Before we could swim, the group would reluctantly gather in the meeting room and sit in a rough semicircle on wooden folding chairs built for people taller than us and the preacher would beg us to save ourselves. He'd go on and on, getting more and more excited. This was nothing new, nothing we hadn't heard every Sunday. He said the same things. *Does he think we have impaired memory? Why doesn't he shut up so we can go down to the lake!* Nothing is ever that easy. I wouldn't have minded if he said anything different. I liked the explanations many preachers used to tie some incomprehensible verse from the Bible to everyday life. But this preacher had a limited capacity for analogy. There was no escape. Flies buzzed drearily in the high rafters, a car would pass, perhaps muffled voices from the gift shop would distract me. Anything.

I thought about my sins: I lied a lot, made up things. I felt guilty about it and promised to stop. I didn't. I couldn't help it. Sometimes I swore like Daddy. I complained if things weren't to my liking, but I don't think anyone liked slimy ooze creeping up their legs. I didn't think that would make my heart black. Maybe it would. I went to the movies on Sunday and read the comics. I hated people sometimes, but got over it. Sometimes I pretended to be sick so I wouldn't have to go to school. But then, I also wanted world peace and everybody to get along and gave dimes for the missions to bring the light to savages and cannibals. I tried not to step on ants and other small crawling things unless they were in my house. Did one set of virtues outweigh one set of vices?

Meanwhile the preacher droned on, exhorted, waved his arms, and thumped the podium. We shifted our fannies on the hard chairs. Through the window the lake gleamed in the sun. We watched as the preacher stopped to mop his face with a white hankie. *Perhaps he'll faint*, I thought. *Is that an evil thought? I'll run for help*, I promised myself.

Eventually we could see that the only way we would get out of the meeting was to be saved. I had already been saved, twice. I didn't need to be saved again. However, one by one, the others got down on their knees beside their chairs. *God*, I thought, *how many times*. Is resentfulness a sin? I hated this rough persistence full of torture, threats, eternal damnation. It was boring.

The rafters were open and heat gathered there in the shallow arch, dropping its weight on us. Through the open windows we could hear the bird music and the water song. *If only he would shut up, we could go swim*. That anguished wish was reflected on all our sweaty little faces.

When Emily Dickinson was a student at Mt. Holyoke, she was the only one who was not saved during the year. I would stare at her picture, that plain little face, a mirror. She had stood strong against them, had not kneeled, had not opened her heart. She had kept it to herself. I saw myself slinking out of my chair, slithering to my knees, a black snake in the water, perhaps that same black snake that had crawled across our yard the day I was born, my omen—scary, but harmless. There are worse sins than the ones on the big ten list, like sinning against yourself. Frequently, I violated that one to get by.

You maintain the character you are born with. I appear to be whatever people want on the outside. That is my gift. I adapt camouflage to protect myself and seem to go with the flow, that current of life everyone seems to be living in but me. But I am the rock sticking out of the water, watching it pass, eroded by its constant swish. That rock is dull and gray. Break it open, inside is a circle of quartz, shades of green and gold. My heart knows no religion it will not invite in.

In the small shop in the rough barnlike building at Heart Lake, a kaleidoscope was for sale, too expensive, but I would roll it around as long as I could and watch each design follow the next, an endless variety, trying to remember if I'd seen this one before, if it marked the beginning of the cycle.

Heart Lake, more a pond than a lake, froze solid in winter. We would tie on our skates and clear the ice out as far as we dared until we could look down and see it clear and black, swept by the wind. It was as frightening as the sound of the summer creatures diving deep. I'd rush back toward the land, terrified of the danger under our feet, so close only a thin glassy film separated us. Did cold change us like it did water into an impermeable window that stood between us and the mysteries of the dark?

Oh, I had big questions. People misunderstood, told me the obvious or the scientific. Water freezes when it's cold. The molecules are slowed. But in my mind the dark glassy covering was a metaphor hiding another world that thrived beneath the thin surface, a slow world filled with dark dreaming.

I think of my heart like that—black glass, slippery and treacherous; it would appear to be solid then dissolve as you stepped forward. I think it had to be, to keep strangers out, keep myself safe, protect what I was from preachers who wanted to add souls to their sermons like scalps to a belt.

When I was a child I spoke and thought as a child, but when I became a woman, I put away childish things. For each parable, a counter proposal. When I childishly misunderstood things or thought the way I had been born into was the only way, I was delighted by difference. I chased after it, followed it down obscure alleys of spirit, drank foreign philosophies like metaphoric cream. All my questions had been asked before. The answers were strung before me like bright beads. When I recognized the pattern, the simplicity of it was so complex, I was delighted—like a kaleidoscope, the pattern shifts.

Emerging Man
Judith Harper, USA
INFLUENCE: SPIRITUALITY (ORIGINAL: JUDAISM)

"I firmly believe that we are all gifted with spiritual genes, inner codes that belong to the very nature of what we are. Every human being has an inner purpose, a meaningful, creative potential, a compass pointing toward fulfillment."

—SØREN HAUGE, Denmark
INFLUENCE: THEOSOPHY

"Everyone is different, so there should be different paths to suit the different temperaments. It is important to find the path that suits oneself, and then to follow it under the guidance of an expert."

—BRAHMACHARINI DIPAMRITA CHAITANYA, France
INFLUENCE: HINDUISM (ORIGINAL: CHRISTIANITY)

"I know I am limited in so many ways. I could not lean on my own understanding, otherwise, I would fail."

—OLUBUNMI GABRIEL OSHO-DAVIES, China (birthplace: Nigeria)
INFLUENCE: PENTECOSTAL CHRISTIANITY (ORIGINAL: TRADITIONAL BELIEFS)

"After an atheistic period in my adolescence, I was soon aware that I could not ignore my spirituality any longer, but also knew that I needed a religion without dogmas, open to free inquiry and the wisdom of the world's religions.

"It is important to follow at least one spiritual path: your own. You may decide to submit your will and conscience to one religious doctrine or dogma, but if you decide to do that, at least be honest to yourself and be aware of your decision and its consequences for you."

—JAUME DE MARCOS, Spain
INFLUENCE: UNITARIAN UNIVERSALISM (ORIGINAL: CATHOLICISM)

"Until I was able to understand how I am connected to the Life Force, the One God, the One Humanity, ME as ME seemed to have no meaning. And that meant no self-worth or understanding. It was important for me to be able to understand how I came to be in this grand scheme of things. Only then would I be able to know where to go from here."

—CECELIA ALPHONSUS, Malaysia
INFLUENCE: NEALE DONALD WALSCH, NATURE, WICCA, OTHERS (ORIGINAL: CATHOLICISM, BUDDHISM)

"I find more comfort in the spiritual way. There are few rewards from dismissing the fact that there is indeed a higher force—a better being. And I need to believe that the struggle that we face every day— whether it be financial or moral—is only a prelude to a better 'end.'"

—MARIANNE LAVALLE-VINCENT, USA
INFLUENCE: CATHOLICISM

Needs

Aaron Holsworth, USA
INFLUENCE: SPIRITUAL QUESTIONS

My mind needs rest, my heart needs comfort, all the air I take in needs to be fully inhaled.
My body needs nourishment, all those I love need to be loved more deeply.
My eyes need a fresh view and my hands need a soft touch. All that I understand, I understand for a reason.
My feet need a clear path my arms need something to care for.
My ears need more powerfully gentle sounds of the ocean. My tongue needs more amazing and wonderful things to taste.
What a wondering and lost soul am I, looking for all those things in one short lifetime.

If I Claim

Michael Hooven, USA

INFLUENCE: SPIRITUALITY, TRUTH AND KNOWLEDGE

If I claim to be a man of God, let me dwell on that which is good and noble in all people. And if one man raises his hand to strike the other, let God show them a greater tolerance as I step between them. But you say to me, what of this wicked doer or that wicked doer? Let me proclaim my righteousness in God by refusing to hate another simply because I was told to. Let me forgive them and set myself free because hate can only be learned. And if you ask where hate comes from, I say only from the past. And if you say that hate separates, I say that separation hates.

I can seek to celebrate the diversity in all of nature, and all of humanity. I can seek to celebrate the diversity in all cultures and in all ways of believing. I can remember words like cohabitation and cooperation and cocreation. I can remember that the sun shines equally on all people. I can remember that the fig tree shares its fruit with all people, regardless of their history, place of origin, or destination. I can observe springtime as a never-ending wave of new growth sweeping around the planet. I can observe winter as the necessary preparation for the new growth to follow.

Meditation

Marco Cuba-Ricsi, USA

3
DARK TIMES
The Influence of Crisis, Disease, Death, or Loss on Spiritual Beliefs

*"Men are disturbed not by things,
but by the view which they take of them."*

—EPICTETUS

The Earthly Death of Diana
Allison Merriweather, USA

The Seed
Terrance L. Burton, USA

It seemed that the sides of my little house I had been building spiritually were about to do more than feel the pressure of the storm, they were about to fall. I didnt understand why the Lord wouldnt have made a better plan for me than this.

I remember being woken up in the middle of the night to find my mother arguing with someone over dope. I thought I was tripping but it was true. It was like this heaviness was put on my back I had no hope in this place, I would turn on the t.v. just to hear something of God and just call out to him to forgive me for what Ive done.

I know I was at my lowest point when someone was telling me God gave me a gift but I need to get smart and get about a hundred or more dollars worth of dope and sell it to get out of that place.

It was wild there cause most of the people that would come into the place knew me as a minister but I wasnt feeling like one because look where Im at. As I lay in my bed one day feeling like every demon in Hell was against me God spoke to me and said

Its eazy to be faithful when nothing is going on in your life thats stressful. Its eazy to minister to people when you know theyre saved, but in a place where no one seems to care its a calling to minister to people that you wouldnt be around or like, its where our Lord is.

So I sucked it up and started to talk to the people more and more about Father Gods Love despite our thinking and ways of belief.

Dying Flowers
Tony Scheuhammer, Canada

The God I Know

Sibusisiwe Nkomo, USA (birthplace: Zimbabwe)

INFLUENCE: SKEPTICISM (ORIGINAL: CHRISTIANITY,
TRADITIONAL AFRICAN BELIEFS)

I denounce the god that killed my mother,
That watched as I had an emotional breakdown,
And still did not bring her back.
I refuse to share my life with a god
Who lives through a book,
And hides behind faith.

Instead I'll live in this bottomless pit of despair,
Where hope and faith are chemical illusions.
I'll find comfort in the empty darkness
And lie awake, waiting for the devil's deception.
Because in my chasm of grief, The Devil's Betrayal
Is better than a god's impotence.

Torn Sleeve

Jeff Leong, Malaysia

INFLUENCE: BORN AGAIN CHRISTIANITY
(ORIGINAL: CHINESE BUDDHISM/TAOISM, ZEN)

See the tear in my sleeve?
My heart used to hang there,
full of passion, dreams and beliefs;

till it got somewhat savvy,
simply much too heavy,
and dropped off.

You can mend sleeves torn apart,
that's easy enough.

Try searching for a lost heart,
God knows, that's really tough!

Consuelo

Tirzo Martha,
Netherlands Antilles

51

Travelogue—Short Stories

Kathryn Gessner, USA
INFLUENCE: TIBETAN BUDDHISM

She gave up caffeine
Took to the road.
Highway 36 to the volcano
Or Chico, California.

Catapulted into a walnut grove
By the owl of her windshield,
She parks, opens the door,
Filling the fields and trees distant
With the *vajra guru* mantra
Expanding off the CD.

The bloodless owl dead in her hands,
Talons curled, wings wide, eyes wide,
She carries to her passenger seat.

She gets that
Someone else will die
Maybe the man from Artesia,
New Mexico, who once taught her
Kundalini fire breath.
Near Grants Pass, Oregon,
He waits out his kidneys.

Maybe the old dog.
Maybe the lilac bush.

Just her and the owl in the seat
Rock on to Chico
With the question.
On repeat the CD rendition moves to *mani*.
Om mani padme hung hri.

She buys a weeping birch
At her destination, white bark peeling,
Plants the birch above the owl's ribs.

Owl

Tuy Nga Brignol, France (birthplace: Vietnam)
INFLUENCE: SPIRITUALITY, CHANNELING,
MEDITATION, PRAYER

Elegy in Fall

Kate Delany, USA

INFLUENCE: SPIRITUALITY, SUFFERING

Tricia, the world's whispering
your soft elegy this season,
to your last work, your hyacinths,
packed safe beneath the cold soil and me,
desperate on these dim afternoons
for the easy half-light of your kitchen table
where we once sat, read parker, mansfield, millay,
planned, waited.

without you, this fall,
I have too much to drink
and nowhere to go, meander
the empty tangle
of familiar streets to park again
by your old darkened home,
waiting for spring, those hyacinths to grow.

Cemetery by Orchid Tree

Joel A. Schlauch, USA

INFLUENCE: ILLNESS, RECOVERY

Fatima Gailani

Afghanistan, political and women's rights activist, president of the Red Crescent Society, spokesperson for the National Islamic Front of Afghanistan, and author of *The Mosques of London*

INFLUENCE: ISLAM (SUNNI SUFI)

Was there a time when you questioned the nature of spirit and how to incorporate it into your life?

I never questioned the existence of God because if I did I would be too empty. But I would not be a human being if I did not question why God allowed some things. When I saw these babies brought to London, burned by napalm bombs, my question to God was *Why was it allowed?* Why was it allowed that another nation [the former Soviet Union] could be so powerful they could drop napalm bombs on our children?

I was caring for a two-month-old baby who had no face, who had no nose, eyelids, or lips, and could not even close his eyes when he was sleeping. Looking at him, I would ask God *Why did you allow such things?* I felt helpless, so I would question God *Why did you make us so helpless?*

Then returning to Afghanistan, I expected that after twenty-four years of war there would be destruction, but when I saw all the vegetation brutally dried up because of seven years of drought, I asked *Why are you doing this to us? Look what is happening. People have destroyed enough, why did you destroy all this?* Starved people had to move from the areas where they had lived for years and years because they could not find a drop of water to drink let alone enough to cultivate anything. I could not blame the Russians, I could not blame the civil war, I could not blame one side or the other side or my neighbors, so my question was to God.

I do not think that these questions are really related to not believing; rather, when you believe in God, really believe in God, then you have quarrels with God also. So I had several episodes of my quarrels with God.

Please describe your personal experience of those questions.

For me it is like having questions of someone very close to you. If you have questions of your mother or father or family, you allow yourself these questions because you know that you are so close they will not be angry with you. I do not question the existence of God. I do not question whether I believe or do not believe.

Desmond Tutu

South Africa, global leader and activist, Nobel Peace Prize Laureate, retired Anglican Archbishop, and author of *God Has a Dream: A Vision of Hope for Our Time*

INFLUENCE: CHRISTIANITY

Was there a time when you questioned the nature of spirit and how to incorporate it into your life?

I have never doubted that God is good and so on. What I would say I called into question frequently was *On whose side are you, God?* I never questioned that God was powerful, that God was loving, but I used to get very angry with God. I used to protest to God when awful things were happening at home and I would say *How in the name of everything that is good can you allow this to happen?* But not question the existence of God or anything of that kind.

Why follow a spiritual path of any kind (as opposed to a particular path)?

It is not just that there is a spiritual hunger, it is how we are made. We have been created as extraordinary things, we are finite creatures who can be satisfied only by the infinite. The great African saint Augustine said "Thou has made us for thyself, and our hearts are restless until they find their rest in thee."

They say in each one of us there is a God-shaped space and only God can fill that space. We often try to find things other than God to satisfy us and we always come up short because only God can ultimately satisfy the deep hunger in us. And so when you say that people are hankering after God, they are just being natural. That is what they should be doing from year one.

Fire

David Collier

INFLUENCE: SPIRITUALITY, NOT RELIGION (ORIGINAL: CHRISTIANITY)

Moving Quietly among Us

Joan Malerba-Foran, USA

Those holy move among us
in quiet, unexpected ways.
Usually they pass quickly
through our lives, spaced
apart and single file,
saying pithy things or
better yet, nothing at all.
Not like those dead—
gathering in noisy numbers
called tragedies. After
a plane crash, when they wash
limp and silent onto shore,
you can't mistake them,
even if for one moment
they appear like lost dolphins.
And whatever the size
of the war, no hole has ever
been dug deep enough
to contain their overflow.
Even a single dead body
clamors to fill whatever
space you have to give it.

No matter how quietly
your mother's spine bent,
how mute your father's form
around the pain of colon cancer,
how satisfied the stillborn
sucking his thumb not five
minutes earlier, one dead
body takes too much space.
Not like the holy, who fast
into flexible reeds and turn
their gaunt cheeks time
and again until we're numb
to their message. How
unexpected the holy are,
moving so quietly among us.
Wouldn't you think they'd make
more noise than the dead?

Divine Guidance
Wanda Harding, USA

Her, Rising

Veneta Masson, USA
INFLUENCE: HEALING ART

Yes there are the memories
like little phylacteries strapped to our minds,
and there are the ways we know our dead
have worked inside us,

when, for example
I touch up my lipstick in public—
  I who never drew attention
  to my mouth
or overpack for a trip—
  I who never gave weight to choice
  only to necessity
or love what she loved—
the beach, the sun—
  I who seek peace
  in the shadows of mountains and trees.

But what is this deep, gurgling laugh
from the well of my throat
that is not me
nor her mark?
What is this laugh
if not her, rising in me?

Is this how souls come back to life—
  in our bodies?
And is this how *they* keep *us* alive—
  with unexpected shocks
  of recognition?

Beseeching the Gods

S. Dolly Malik, USA

INFLUENCE: SPIRITUALITY

I stepped out into the balmy September night. The wind was the gentle breeze of a late summer evening. The crickets chirping in a nearby bush almost drowned out the background roar of the expressway traffic. I felt the cold splash of a couple of errant raindrops, their cold dampness a sharp contrast to the humid air.

Yes, I thought suddenly. I yearn for the heavens to simply open up, pouring torrents of water from the sky. A desire that the gods, themselves, cry the tears that I have not been able to shed. How I wanted the skies to roll into the pitch-blackness not seen since the day that Jesus of Nazareth cried out at his Father's abandonment. I beseeched Shiva, the god of destruction, to release a torrential flood so powerful as to drown out the species that allowed Satan to cultivate this incomprehensible hatred in our midst. I invoked the thunder of Zeus and the lightening of Jupiter to rid us poor humans of such evil, knowing full well that their expressions of wrath would be a pale reflection of the anger and pain raging within me.

The wind remained gentle. The air was heavy with moisture. The gray clouds overhead stubbornly retained the splashes of white. Streaks of the setting sun reflected off the thick wall of clouds, creating an eerie yellow-orange glow. By now the frogs had joined in the chorus initiated by the crickets. Standing, breath held, within the unchanged whispers of the night, I knew my prayers to the gods had not been answered.

Why do you not speak, I demanded of them. Do not the horrific acts of this time demand a catastrophic repudiation of the evil that has been allowed to fester? Answer me, oh Almighty gods. Answer me. Or, at least let me see that you, the gods, like we miserable mortals, also weep in your anguish over what we, your children, have become.

Silver Chain

Robin Greene, USA

INFLUENCE: BUDDHISM (ORIGINAL: JUDAISM)

Perhaps it was the beggar's bowl I carried
   invisibly
this morning—my training cup, tipped to receive
what I must accept, in the holy practice of having
and letting go.

   I knew better
but this morning I kept my eyes averted,
my attention unfixed so that I couldn't
see the washed acrylic sky lower its white
blanket as dawn appeared and I shuffled
down the driveway to retrieve the newspaper,

couldn't feel the cool damp of its plastic
as I slid the paper roll from its foreskin,
couldn't hear the muted bands of morning

ring from the shadowed kitchen before I flicked
on the light. I didn't wonder: *what life is this
   before me?*
Didn't extend and offer my bowl to the textured
silence, nor realize nor appreciate its gift.

   Instead, I got caught
in the worrying of a silver chain I found knotted
in my bathrobe's pocket, and somehow my
   wooden
bowl, though invisible, got misplaced. In the drift
of hours that was morning, I spent my time
with fingers grating against links.

Dream

Natela Grigalashvili, Georgia

Diptych

Damien Scott, USA

INFLUENCE: CATHOLICISM

PART I: ISAIAH 35:2

Let the desert bring forth flowers like the jonquil,
Let it rejoice and sing for joy.
The glory of Lebanon is bestowed on it,
The splendor of Carmel and Sharon;
They shall see the glory of the Lord,
The splendor of our God.

And I, the brown-robed one
Who stands and stays—
    Silent in the morning cool
    Beneath the green and blue of day—
Watch my friend depart alone.
Turning, walking, thinking
Now I have left home.

There were so many loved
Or so it seemed to me—
    To them perhaps.
But there was always one to whom I turned
To share such different lives;
And he—
    "But you, my other self,"
    the psalmist cries—
Has left the home
I left so long ago.

I, the brown-robed one,
Sitting silent prayers
Before the wakened past
That will not be again
    And maybe never was.
Faces long forgot and names.
Kneeling, rising, hearing voices
Yet recalling pain,
I still feel pain—
    A different kind of love.

I do not know,
In seeing one depart,
If *Nunc dimittis* or *Ita missa est*
Is best,
Allowing for it all to fall
Behind green eyes,
The brown-robed one.

And maybe for a moment
I let myself be lost—
Like once the eighteen years were tossed aside—
And remembering the bitterness of gain,
I relish now
The peacefulness of loss.

PART II: THERE IS A SONG

Twenty Years after Isaiah 35:2

And I, the brown-robed one
Who sit and wait
Beneath gray sky beside gray sea
And watch my life unpart.

Where once the blue and green of spring
Showed forth prophetic buds of growth
And bursts of life beneath the bark
Swelled to wink at tree tips' end,
Now leaves and cones alike but fall
And I, the brown-robed one,
Sit and watch it all.

What did I then expect?
I do not know,
Have burned the journals of that long-off day
And cannot bring to mind
The dreams that moved and kept me there to stay.
I lived the life,
I found the questions
    Not the plan.

And worst of it,
Oh, worst of it
Is having come thus far
And found myself at home—
    I'm not at home.
There is no home.

There is a song beneath my mind,
Music unsung
But so unlike the song
I thought to sing.
It is not words,
Though words my favored sons.
It is not words.

Sitting silent prayers,
Wordless prayers,
Prayerless prayers.
The scape is clean, not ash,
    Is white serene,
     Quite serene.
Twenty years to learn
That life's not in the bud
But in the falling seed.

I fall.

Train Station
Ana Maria Marques, Portugal

*"Life is the accumulation of all experiences, good or bad,
that make us see things from a different perspective and catch
hold of the inner meanings in our lives.*

*"How and why I got the cancer, I don't care much about any more;
I thank God for the new life that has been bestowed on me.
What still motivates me today, every day: I tell myself that
I wasn't given a second chance at life for nothing."*

—RIZWAN FAROOQ, Kingdom of Bahrain
INFLUENCE: SPIRITUALITY, SURVIVING CANCER

*"In 1998 when an outbreak [of violence between religious groups] occurred
in Nigeria, I considered it spiritual turmoil by demons and decided I had
to seize the practice of a religion. A spiritual person should be devoted to God
and detest war. Spirit in war is different than spirit in pacifism.
Since I was born into a Christian home, went to Islamic schools, and grew up
in a traditional environment, I see spiritualism as a thing of heaven
to provide peace for terrestrial beings. We must live in cohesion. To practice
pantheism is to re-create peace for people. It is a religion of no bias."*

—WALE AJAKAYE, Nigeria
INFLUENCE: PANTHEISM (ORIGINAL: CHRISTIANITY; ISLAM, TRADITIONAL BELIEFS)

The Confession

T. Ashok Chakravarthy, India

INFLUENCE: HINDUISM

When the dreams of childhood
Were about to flourish
You turned them into a nightmare.

When the charms of youth
Were about to delight
You scratched me without mercy.

When the buds of childish love
Were about to blossom
You plucked them in a fit of rage.

When I was set to sail off
For a brief cruise in life's boat
You capsized it with the tempest of uncertainty.

Without a spark of hope or trace of luck
Lo destiny! Why do you hunt me
Without any respite or mercy.

If life itself is a deceit
O destiny, I salute you for the devotion
Tired and vexed, I concede my defeat.

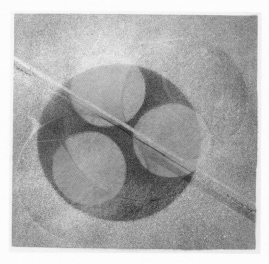

Seven Sacred Numbers: Octad

Ray Pierotti, USA

INFLUENCE: SPIRITUALITY, CATHOLICISM, MORMONISM

Needle

Stephanie L. Morehead, USA

INFLUENCE: SPIRITUAL AWAKENING, PAIN, GRIEF

No, I am not the same
Over a thousand moons
Have passed
While I have been
Pulling threads
And coming undone
I grasp the needle
With trembling hand
To stitch my parts
Madness hits with
Such stealth
I want to blame
The sky
Curse its name
Damn the moon
But I know now
It starts right here
In the quiet space

In Search of the Goddess

Lillian Comas, USA

INFLUENCE: SPIRITUALITY, HEALING

The monkey's cry pierced my heart. The man in front of me screamed, losing his balance as the animal tore his shirt. "It found my candy offerings to Kali," he said, wiping his wounds.

I got dizzy staring at the bloody floor. "Human blood is her favorite libation," our guide said. "But we can't sacrifice anymore. The government prohibited us and her statue tilted its head."

"Is the goddess angry?" I asked, gasping for air. "Of course, she no longer feeds on her children." Originally, Kali's priests used human blood for *bindis*, the red dots Hindus wear on their foreheads. Women offered their menstrual fluid to represent the opening of their third eye. Listening to the guide, my flow began, renewing my dread of female blood. Before meeting Kali, it had mysteriously stopped in front of the Jain temple with the sign prohibiting entrance to menstruating women.

"How do they know we're bleeding?" asked a voice with feminist fervor. "They smell you," I joked; the women in our group laughed in conspiracy. In defiance, we took our photographs in front of the sign.

Adorned for a wedding, the temple screamed femaleness. Young women dressed in red, magenta, and crimson saris kissed voluptuous female idols. While girls placed flower petals like glistening rubies on the floor, older women brewed exotic concoctions that awakened our appetites.

A scarlet aura impregnated the air while monkeys feasted on candy. The Black One is bloodthirsty. I saw her face as soon as I entered the altar. Her tilted expression oscillated between fury and love. Enthralled, I requested consecration. Her priest opened my third eye. I saw darkness out of light: *Daughter*. I turned to answer the call; Kali stared back at me.

☙

I found my maternal ancestry in Andalusía. People treated me like blood, using the endearing voice reserved for family. My first night in Granada I ate dinner in front of a mirror, or so I thought, until my husband Fred told me that the woman in the nineteenth-century painting looked just like me.

Nataraja Mandala

Youjia Song, Australia

INFLUENCE: HINDUISM, TIBETAN BUDDHISM, PSYCHEDELIC APPROACH

"I saw your face many times in Andalusía," Mami said on her deathbed. Hurt that I wouldn't have children, she struggled to stay alive for the birth of her son's child, but died a month later asphyxiated in blood vomit. To exorcise my pain, I invoked Kali, brandishing a bloodstained sword and dripping human head, her foot on her husband Shiva. Her necklace of heads represents our false identities; she brutally removes each one so we can find our divinity. Losing my mortal mother, I found a divine one.

Watching daily *gitana* movies, I longed to be a flamenco dancer. A favorite, *Blood Wedding*, depicts the central role of blood among gypsies. Each dance a sacrifice, mortals make offerings to their goddess. I decided to pay respects to the *Virgen de la Macarena*, patroness of bullfighters, who rules over swords, blood, and death. During Holy Week, her acolytes parade her statue, following the path of Jesus' blood through the streets of Sevilla. She is the *Virgen de los morenos*, the dark-skinned *gitanos* who brought Kali from India, transforming her into the Madonna.

One afternoon, I invited myself to a gypsy wedding. The bridesmaids marched like vestal attendants, smiling and flirting through their black mantillas. The bride appeared in a red dress, dancing down the aisle in the midst of *Olé mi niña*. Her stomping feet cadenced the music as her sinuous arms hypnotized us. "*La novia* dances for Her," the woman next to me said.

The groom waited at the altar in supplication, watching with the intensity of a toreador about to kill the bull. When she reached him, *la novia* pulled a dagger from between her breasts. Taking his hand, she cut the palm, *olés* erupting in the church, pierced her flesh, and blended their blood in a flamenco clap. She then placed the bloodstained blade at the Madonna's feet. The *¡Viva los novios!* transformed the wedding into a *fiesta de toros*, its pathos reminiscent of a baptism and a funeral.

ॐ

"*Comas*, that's Catalán," our taxi driver declared in Barcelona. "I came back after five hundred years," I said. In less than a year I traced my roots from Andalusía to Africa to Cataluña. After a train ride, I jumped into a funicular full of Filipino pilgrims engaged in a spellbinding incantation as we swung back and forth between rocks and sky. The hypnotic journey ended at a basilica carved out of steep peaks.

"Two lines, one for Mass, the other for the Madonna," a man shouted. *La Moreneta*, the Dark One, was nesting her son on her lap, the world-sphere in her hand. Video-taping Monserrat, Kali stared back at me. Confused, I forgot to perform the ritual, lost my balance, and fell down. "Touch her," a man behind me commanded. I retraced my steps. *Daughter*. I felt blessed, caressed her globe.

The next day we left for Katmandu. During the trip Fred noticed my *bindi*. We tried to explain how it survived strenuous showers. It's stigmata, I realized.

"Nepal's first tourist attraction is Mount Everest; its second is Kumari, the living goddess," our guide explained. "Some say she's Parvati, others say she's Durga, but I believe she is Kali." Selected from a special caste of girls, Kumari must meet thirty-two strict physical and mystical requirements and her horoscope must complement Nepal's king, believed to be Shiva's personification. The candidates are gathered in the temple hall, staying the entire night with the blood and carcasses of slaughtered animals. The girl who withstands the ritual with a regal composure becomes the living goddess. When Kumari begins to menstruate or accidentally loses a lot of blood, another girl takes her place.

"Can we see her?" I asked, but was told that Kumari only leaves her temple six times a year. Disappointed, I went to a Buddhist temple and prayed for my dead. An image of painted eyes on the top of the *stupa* appeared during my meditation. Encircled with kohl to ward off evil spirits and protect children, Asian eyes followed me everywhere. The same eyes showed in Kumari postcards.

A bacchanalia of images, sounds, and fragrances assaulted me. Suddenly, a commotion: a caravan—horns blowing, music playing, cries ripping the air—carried a throne. Instinctively, I chased it, recording everything. A beautiful girl with painted eyes emerged. She stared back at me as her attendants lifted her from the chariot (she is not to touch the ground with her feet) and carried her into the temple. "You're blessed," the guide told me later. "On your first day you find the living goddess."

∽✺∽

The first week of my Asian pilgrimage, I dreamt that my brother was dead. Fred reminded me that in *espiritismo*, this signifies a birth. Indeed, my niece had been born prematurely. My third eye had witnessed her arrival. Our trip to Atlanta was pregnant with excitement and distress; meeting Antonia was saddened by my mother's death. David and his wife asked me to be godmother; I accepted on the condition of avoiding Catholic classes. No priest would agree with my request.

"Who will bless Antonia? She'll go to limbo if she dies unbaptized," I whispered. The first time I saw her, I searched for my mother's face. Carrying Puerto Rican, British, Filipino, African, Hawaiian, Spanish, Chinese, German, and Taino genes, the baby looked like a poster for multiculturalism. Videotaping my goddaughter, Kumari stared back at me.

Metamorphosis of a Woman

Lara Chauvin, Canada

INFLUENCE: WOMANHOOD, PASSIONATE CYCLES; FIRE,
DARKNESS, DEPTH, HOPE, FEMININITY . . .

Hospital with My Sister Visiting

Meghan Adler, USA

INFLUENCE: UNITARIANISM, REFORM JUDAISM, BUDDHISM

(ORIGINAL: CATHOLICISM, JUDAISM, UNITARIAN UNIVERSALISM, QUAKERISM)

It isn't the IV line or me
at the window feeling winter at my fingers.
Isn't the sound of heart monitors beeping
or smells of vomit, bed pans, ammonia
but the light out there—genuine light
and a large maple tree,
wind making it move, come alive.
It is the shining of sun on certain patches
of bark harkening: orange and gold.

And then, as if God has been listening,
a white plastic bag, clean and empty,
blows across my window,
flutters from limb to limb
until it hooks a high branch
and stays put
while its body floats and fills.
I touch my swollen face,
feel it throbbing.
See, Sarah. Things hold.

Time Passing

Reneé Dumont, USA

INFLUENCE: SEVENTH-DAY ADVENTIST CHURCH, SABBATH KEEPER

(ORIGINAL: BIBLE, SPIRITUAL LEADERS)

The Gift of Pain

Jeff Hutner, USA
INFLUENCE: BUDDHISM, TAOISM

I was lying in bed about four in the morning when I decided to ask my pain why it was there. The answer I received was quick and profound: *I am the pain of the separation of who you are and who you're pretending to be.*

When I look back on the physical and emotional pain I experienced, I see them not as bad memories to be erased but as personal evolutionary drivers to be celebrated. They led me on a powerful journey toward my authentic self, for which I will be forever grateful. I have also come to appreciate the idea that much of the pain of our world comes from people who have stopped dreaming, listening, and acting on their inner urges, inklings, and passions. Far too many of us have interiorized that critical voice that once told us *you're not good enough* or *that's a stupid idea that will never work*.

In the End

Choon Huat Tan, Singapore
INFLUENCE: CHRISTIANITY

I've often wondered,
When the grave is my final resting place,
Why life? What for?

So I searched,
And finally found,
A hope beyond.

Lost and Found

Gilbert Allen, USA

I hadn't been playing.
Just sauntering
along, a sunny afternoon,
a shortcut to
somewhere—despite
my motion, what newspapers
proclaim an innocent
bystander. But the only

one who'd fit.

So they lowered
me though
the frame
of the awning
window
of the basement
of the ruined
schoolhouse

and let go.

My feet struck the earth
six feet below the earth
they'd come from.
The air hovered, so full
of dust and light
that dust and light
seemed the same.
So I could see—

inside a bookcase

lying like a forefather
lost in his longest nap—
the foul ball, horsehide
unraveled, dark
as a spoiled apple
hardly worth saving.
And after I'd pitched
it up, they thanked me,

laughed, and left.

The next year the suburbs
would reach out with their long
manicured fingers. The whitewashed
rubble would be razed
and resurrected, miraculous
as new money. But this
wasn't next year.
This was hours

and hours

among the bindings
of damp books I couldn't
read, among desks with dry
inkwells, and those cracked
blackboards so small even *my* hands
could hold them—all stained
with stale incense
only half chalk.

These walls weren't going anywhere.

As I longed through their glass
teeth at the lowering
sun, I knew I'd be here
forever, in that new, old dark,
so frightened I wasn't even
frightened—just lost
within the false certainty
of silence.

So, like a perfect student,

I sat at the nearest desk
and slept. I don't remember
who got me out, or when,
or why, although
it must have happened.
I never asked, and now
there is no one
to ask—only a beautiful house

no decent man or woman

can afford. But I'd like
to think my saviors
and my imprisoners
the same—lost
as the child put there
forty years ago, lost
as that other child
more or less

brought back.

Manhattan Bridge #1 (1994)

John Ferry, USA

INFLUENCE: PRESBYTERIANISM

4
BEAUTY AND MYSTERY
How Nature, Love, Birth, and Creativity
Affect Spirituality

"The most beautiful thing we can experience is the mysterious."

—ALBERT EINSTEIN

Spiral

Tony Scheuhammer, Canada

The River

Patricia Hill, USA

INFLUENCE: NONE (ORIGINAL: ROMAN CATHOLICISM)

The soul has found its body—and puzzles out the confluence of ligament and bone, the lattice of possibility and intent. Move the hand, so, and ponder the mind behind it. Like water leaving its high mountain, the body rushes to its own salt sea in endless conversation with itself.

Where is the soul in all this? Is it the white birch leaning dangerously over the gorge, tenacious and beautiful? Is it the white birch fallen, caught, and rushing under the watchful presence of rock and sky? To stand apart and see oneself drowned, to drown and see oneself standing apart, can the soul do all this? Leave it. You cannot dissect the river, no matter how much you want to know. The luminous sand beneath your feet will not tell you. The flat rock will not tell you. Neither will the sequined trout, the flies jigging at the water's skin, filament of spider flung at your face. For all the noise and congregation here, you are left as dumb as you ever were. The river proceeds without you, without the part of you ankle-deep in mud, mouth agape, eye squinting from too much light.

*"As long as you keep questing, staying with the question,
spirit will guide you directly to the answers. The challenge is to live it,
to begin to build your spiritual muscles. Work and discipline is the next stage.
That's the challenge I work with now: living what I teach and believe,
going from **knowing about** to actually **being** it."*

—REV. HOWARD E. CAESAR, USA
INFLUENCE: UNITY, UNIVERSAL SPIRITUAL TEACHINGS (ORIGINAL: LUTHERAN CHURCH)

Pilot
Arturo Rubio Garcia, Mexico

Just a Thought

Bibek Bhandari, Nepal

Let's make peace our religion
Unity our god
Let prayers flow in form of love
Harmony being a sacred hymn.

Climbing Mountains

Rayn Roberts, South Korea (birthplace: USA)

INFLUENCE: BUDDHISM

Out of breath, but not energy, I tire on the upward path,
Stop to see where I am. The summit's not far, but I need water.

It is the taste of spring, taste of April I take, the icy-sweet clean
Can-anything-be-so-pure snowmelt rushing right out of the earth.

This is how I want to be, clean and clear, no phone TV house or car
No worn-out concept, dead-end dogma, news of the dead or war—

Merton had his seven-story mountain, but was a monk. I aspire
Only to know myself and poetry. That, too, is a mountain worth the climb:

To long for, wander out and look for the miracle in the mundane
The unexpected blessing in contradictions, the calm fox napping

A hare hopping by unharmed, the globe spinning from light to dark
In a field of floating stars, sparks . . . rising from a campfire,

The echo of a waterfall . . .
That is what I want, not to get away
But get closer to what I need most and love, a place
Where the many faces of the mountain are one, where I sit
Allow the toil and grief of life to flow out of my mind, out of my body

Drain into the earth like water, and leave me for good.

Gathering

Joan Malerba-Foran, USA

The quick clucking
of early morning musings
as I unlatch the shed door
and step across the sill.
Here, where light enters
only through parting slats,
an audience of hens startle—
hurtle from perch,
surge out in a ruckus of feathers.
Clattering over fences,
they descend into damp fields,
carrying small criticisms
into tall grass.

A row of rumpled nests steam
along the length of one wall.
One by one I gather eggs,
pressing them between layers
of straw in a pail once silver,
dark warmth filling cool cup of palm.
Shells click with a sound
delicate and crucial as marble
chips chiseled, fallen away, left
behind by an artist's hand

for what's art if not that
which is left behind?
A gathering and reordering
of the ordinary—
Egg composed and presented
upon a trust of straw.
Mountain bursting and turning
upon the dais Earth.
Moon hurled and hooked
upon a calculated heaven.
What's art if not the residue
of a deliberate miracle?

Ancient Stream

Juliette Lagenour, USA

Julia Cameron

USA, award-winning author of *The Artist's Way* and *The Vein of Gold*, journalist, and theologian
INFLUENCE: TRIBAL ROMAN CATHOLICISM, CREATIVITY, SPIRITUALITY

Was there a time when you questioned the nature of spirit and how to incorporate it into your life?

The period that I remember as being most full of questions was a period during my adolescence when I was in a conventional Catholic school, and was myself reading theologians further afield. I found that the conventional teachings I was being given in the classroom didn't mesh with my own explorations.

What were the major questions you were dealing with?

I think I had difficulty believing in the *pettiness* of the God I was being taught to believe in; there was such an emphasis on God's paying attention to what we did wrong, and so little emphasis on God being involved with larger issues. I was reading Paul Tillich, who spoke of God as the ground of being, and I was reading Teilhard de Chardin, and there was simply no place in the conventional Catholic girlhood for such far-reaching questioning.

Please describe your personal experience of those questions.

I remember my adolescence as being dark, with a feeling of being misunderstood. I was, in fact, sent to a psychiatrist because of my spiritual questioning. The psychiatrist I was sent to was a nun, and she was quite farseeing. She listened to my angst and said there's nothing wrong with you except that you're quite bright.

What led you in the direction of developing answers for yourself?

When I was twenty-nine years old, I realized that I was an alcoholic, and that I had to get sober. I was taught that Carl Jung had said that the only cure for alcoholism was spirituality. His expression was *"spiritus contra spiritum"*—spirit versus spirits; and so, sort of under a death threat that if I didn't get spiritual I would drink again, I began seeking spiritual answers.

What was it like to realize you might be able to resolve these questions for yourself?

I feel that spirituality is a daily issue. I take comfort in my faith, but I always wish I had more faith. I remember among my friends some older people who have a great comfortability in their belief system. On any given day I might wake up feeling that my spiritual tank is low, and when that happens I reach out to other people who have more faith than I do. I ask for prayers, I go for a walk, and when I walk I talk to my higher power and ask for guidance. I often take myself to the page and ask for guidance, and then listen and write out what I hear. So, for me, it's an ongoing, evolving process rather than one in which I sit with some satisfying comfort.

Can you describe why it was important to find answers to these questions?

I have two things to say about it: first was the knife blade of my alcoholism, which made me afraid of drinking again unless I could find a workable faith; and second was my quest for creativity, and my belief that creativity is a spiritual issue—that it takes faith to try to create. I needed to find a level of faith that would allow me to work. I began to work with the idea that creativity wasn't my asset; it was rather more that I was a conduit or a channel for a larger creative power to work through me; as I became more open to inspiration, my writing sort of settled down, and I became more productive.

Why follow a spiritual path of any kind (as opposed to a particular path)?

It's interesting: I travel to teach a great deal, and in my travels I meet people from many different spiritual persuasions—Buddhist, Hindi, Baha'i, Wiccan. I find that all spiritual paths do lead us home. That if we have devoted ourselves to a spiritual path, there tends to be an open-mindedness and a joyfulness, a sort of lightness, that I find very attractive. I, for example, am friends with one of the nuns that I went to high school with back in the "dark days;" now that forty years have passed, we're quite close to each other, and I will ask her to pray for my intention. She reads my books and tells me that she thinks I'm doing well, which is very encouraging.

Do you identify primarily with one spiritual group, and is this the one you were introduced to as a child?

I don't identify with a particular spiritual path. I would not say I am a practicing Roman Catholic; I would say I am a *tribal Roman Catholic*—that I still am probably more closely affiliated with that than any other path. I read in a wide variety of areas: I love the work of Thich Nhat Hanh, I love Rumi's poetry. . . . Frequently my book *The Artist's Way* is singled out as a Buddhist book or a Sufi book or a Christian book. It seems to mesh with the spiritual path of the reader. So I find that for myself, creativity itself is a spiritual path. I've been on it nearly forty years now, and so I have to say that I think of *The Artist's Way* as a spiritual path in and of itself, not that it precludes other orientations.

Not Stopping for Death

Stephen Mead, USA

INFLUENCE: SURREALISM, EXPRESSIONISM

Portal, the sun is an entrance,
Heaven's keyhole
Rising, setting,
The same mirror to behold
Daily different,
& we, its reflection
As much as any body of water.
Look, feel warmth.
You will not go blind.

Row, the wide waters
Vaporous, interplanetary,
The marsh
In will-o'-the-wisp
Aurora borealis movement . . .
Love, how to cross over
& find you?
I lay down my oars,
Rest invisible & still,
Coast into trust.

In the distance
Storms bash bridges
As dams spilling over,
But the bridges remain whole
As our tidal river of blood
The moon pulls & pulls,
Calling tempests, calling calm.
Ramparts lay down
Strong as the gusts.

Surf curled. Prophetic, ancient
Mariner of liquid salt,
This majestic arc, serpent
Foamed, a crash of hush
Sucking, bubbling back,
Tossing spray
Brine of dragon's breath
To teach us of our Mother's power,
The passion of first birth.

Truth, delusion,
The magical dance,
A glance over shoulders,
We hold onto each other,
Not stopping for death.

Still, with what hooves,
Will the Apocalypse approach?
Will it trample without mercy
Through smoke & flame?

Show us the pale
Riderless horse of compassion
On the Last Judgment Day.

Show us the grove, benchless,
Beneath the red light,
To slow us on our journey.

Will there then come the altarpiece
Foretelling of heaven?
Will there be, on the left,
The angel of emerald wings?
Will there be the hourglass bearer
Displaying the time?
On the right, from white veils,
What roses are dropping?

Love, there have been other timekeepers,
Guardians from the first dawn.

They are quiet. They are knowing.
They shimmer with kindness.

Love, now is the hour.
Do not be afraid.

Neptunian Cavern

Hélène Cardona, USA (birthplace: France)

INFLUENCE: DREAMS, NATURE, MEDITATION, YOGA, SHAMANIC JOURNEYS, MUSIC

I get attached to things to live
  the way darkness gets attached to light,
I let them come to me,
  it takes a while to remove assumptions.
I marvel at travels in air balloons,
  finding my place in the world.
Every day prepares for death,
  I let paths overlap,
a magician's recipe to produce desire,
  knowing when to be visible or invisible.
The transition from the dream is imperceptible,
  a whisper on a stringed instrument.

I reach the bottom of the ocean to retrieve coral,
  a flower animal extending myself to thrive.
The rain hasn't come yet.
  Storms brew at the prow,
force me into stillness,
  a white tulip resting on open lilies.
Be willing to sweep the floor,
  feed from the sediment of the river,
carve shadows burned into ground,
  craft ghost figures out of mud.
Art is perpetual rebirth,
  the way we choose to express ourselves,
    the way we take directives from God.

Time Traveler (Soul Mate)

Marco Cuba-Ricsi, USA

INFLUENCE: ASTRAL PROJECTION

Seasoning

Sarah Anne Shope, USA

INFLUENCE: SPIRITUALITY (AFTER RELIGION)

After decades
of skimming across the surface of this earth,
never taking or being exactly sure
to whom you are giving, you've told God
time and again, you simply will not
play this game to its apogee.

Yet, deep in July you come to know
the feeling of butter melting into bread,
that warming,
until skimming turns to gliding
and you can't imagine
if you are butter or bread.

Deep in summer
you decline the game of dare,
you are grateful just to be,
and so pleased you are not absent.

Then, in a gentle nip of cold
you soon begin to wonder
how autumn will be,
how you will be,
and what is going to be
come winter.

Only I

Emily Veinglory, USA/Canada/Scotland (birthplace: New Zealand)

INFLUENCE: SECULAR HUMANISM, ATHEISM (ORIGINAL: CHRISTIANITY)

Sea gulls, flying, seem white
beneath the hills' dark brow
and black above.

Sheep graze the frosty meadow,
while golden sun paints
the hills above.

Winter is fickle here . . .
beautiful as a dying thing,
for those with faith in resurrection.

Sun and birds see over the horizon:
sheep don't care.

Only I am stranded here.

Joy

Michelle Anne Burke, South Africa

INFLUENCE: THE NATURAL WORLD (ORIGINAL: NONE)

Seabrook Park

Linda Walsh, USA

INFLUENCE: BUDDHISM

(ORIGINAL: CATHOLICISM)

From the Last Week of Summer

Jnana Hodson, USA

INFLUENCE: QUAKERISM, YOGA (ORIGINAL: EVANGELICAL UNITED BRETHREN CHURCH)

In a suitable helpmeet
all of one's emotions
are acknowledged

and turned or returned.
Summer night
silence

includes crickets
or flames.
We finally hear

distilling
that's still
still.

Oppositions reconcile
back into harmony.
Self-centered

silence is unnerving.
Holy silence
centers into calm.

Butter, vinegar, a squeeze
of lemon: everything straight,
simple, not faded but pushing

to individual limits,
our fullest self: fireworks
falling toward earth, toward

a place where we'll hear snow
landing in the garden
when we order seed.

A Very Quiet Thing, Magnetism (Swirling)

Ronald Dahl, Mexico (birthplace: USA)

INFLUENCE: TAOISM (ORIGINAL: CHRISTIAN SCIENCE)

Certain kinds of fantasies
attract me or elude me,
matters of heart
as well of mind,
like playing with a pair
of magnets,
alluring shapes
in the foggy
atmosphere
of childhood (like it was/is).

Yet here the residue
of filings sit lightly
on this page
forming eccentric
concentric patterns
apparent upon
the surface
luring imagination
as to what was
or can possibly be (beneath/within).

Of course what was
is no longer, become
by now but residue,
matters of a mind
toying with patterns
filed fine like steel,
loosely, yet
orderly, undulating
on the surface
of the soul (that then, whatever now).

The patterns can be
mesmerizing as they
drift upon the page,
noticing that part
of things,
seemingly organized,
coherent in space
like sheet music
patiently waiting
for the instruments (& the fine tuning).

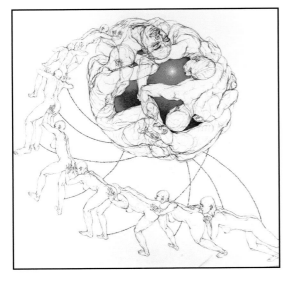

String of Beads 40

Sol Kjøk, USA (birthplace: Norway)

INFLUENCE: BUDDHISM (ORIGINAL: LUTHERAN
STATE CHURCH, NONRELIGIOUS HOME)

The Moment of Knowing

Marie S. Abaya, USA

INFLUENCE: MEDITATION, NATURE, LAND AUTHENTIC MOVEMENT (ORIGINAL: CATHOLICISM)

Up until that point, I did not believe, spent thirty-five years on earth, estranged from living. I often felt dismayed that this was my body, this was my life, and I had to move it.

My name, Abaya, represents the Hindu mudra, palm up facing out, "fearlessness." I loved that confirmation to continue without fear in this life that was not mine.

I found something one day. The alternate meaning of that mudra: Renunciation. Pema Chodron often spoke of it. But now it was mine. My responsibility. Why wasn't it there before? I was holding myself back, resisting life. I had to renounce that disbelief.

The early morning air was sharp as always, but a mistlike fog gently draped over the Douglas-fir hillsides laced with young aspen stands. I had never been this route and relished the mountain scenery with an air of melancholy. I thought of the night before, at the brewpub, saying good-byes. I felt a tightening in my chest, a sadness of leaving, bringing a flow of blurry tears. The early fall sun was breaking through the cold mist in a scattering across the mountains to the west. Then I looked at the pain clearly, and saw it was the pain of being connected, of living and loving. Not the pain I was so familiar with. I was not alone on this earth anymore, in this madness, with this beauty. The pain turned to joy as I physically felt the tightness lift and my heart open and fill my chest with golden warmth. I felt it, the world, the belief, the bond, the grounding, the union, the release.

I cannot explain why it took me so long to get here, why all my study, meditation, art, and vision had not brought me the solace to overcome. This fleeting moment had magic. It gave me lightness and clarity and maturity. Maybe I earned this light, at last ready to give up the struggle. I carry it with me as a talisman of all the energies of the universe connecting together to call me back and claim me and bind me and remind me of the deep significance of my life.

Ferris Wheel

Lori L. Desautels, USA

INFLUENCE: SPIRIT, DIVINE INTELLIGENCE, FAMILY . . . (ORIGINAL: FEARFUL BEARDED-GOD-IN-THE-SKY CHRISTIANITY)

Squares of a quilt we observed from above. The ethereal view outlined the colors and shapes that moved through the delicate fabric I had stumbled upon before. What is this blanket for and who will it comfort?

"You are quiet Mommy," my daughter whispered.

I listened to the heavy chimes of the cathedral bells lulling my memory inside the distant past. These same bells had brought me to my knees so long ago as the cells of my existence recognized and responded, aching for the quiltmaker.

Please begin again . . .

The chipped yellow paint and the clanking of the torn leather seats did not disturb the scent of cherry tobacco permeating the cubicle of space where my grandfather and I ventured. Our hands held firmly as we jerked to a swinging stop on the top of my world.

A world of theater, actors, lights, and the perfect stage create the setting where pain and joy are sliced and revealed in fragments of time.

She wasn't aware she was summoning quilt squares. Rearranging the pieces to fit inside the whole, she continued to play and examine each one. The quilt spun shadows under the setting sun.

Squinting, I spotted squares that were unfinished and threadbare, pleading to be pricked and sewn into the perfection of this design. The sound of squeaking metal shot us onto the precipice overlooking the material that awaited the weaving of all times.

Those around us did not feel or anticipate the jolt, for they slept, nurturing the illusion from center stage.

The Woman Who Married a Tree

Vivian Faith Prescott, USA

INFLUENCE: SAAMI HERITAGE

Lunatic

Peggy Heinrich, USA

INFLUENCE: SPIRITUALITY

There's a reason to be on this train,
to have this slice of time
to read this Chekhov story

with its theme of marriage growing cold,
to go where I'll be heading
from the terminal, to encounter

those I will encounter. Scalp
tingles at this sport: reading purpose
into every act, discounting chance.

That man across the aisle—
who might he have been,
not in his current form but . . .

. . . lunatic to play this game
that may be greater than a game,
full of cosmic messages and meaning.

Without Name

Ronya Shvachka, Israel (birthplace: Ukraine)

INFLUENCE: MY SON (ORIGINAL: CHRISTIANITY)

Birth

Elena Retfalvi, Spain

Suspended in time,
Hidden in a cocoon woven of different threads:
Red for blood, shimmering white for innocence—
You are just about to enter this world incognito
Burning clandestine comet
With a misty tail of destiny.
Would anyone ever know
What strange dreams caress these neatly shut eyelids,
What secret knowledge leaves a ghost of a smile
On those silent lips?

With Child

Laurie L. Ludes, USA
INFLUENCE: CHRISTIANITY,
JESUS CHRIST

Solano

T. Geronimo Johnson, USA

INFLUENCE: TIBETAN BUDDHISM, CATHOLICISM,
J. KRISHNAMURTI (ORIGINAL: CATHOLICISM,
CHARISMATIC CHRISTIANITY)

I award you my hand
and my tiny urges,
to bathe
us in the perfume of ferocious hope
drink slowly,
and laugh at the blind,
    who speak only in fear,
for ours is a sail called home
    in Solano
to greet the blushing angels
remember,
it is love, not gravity
that binds us
all

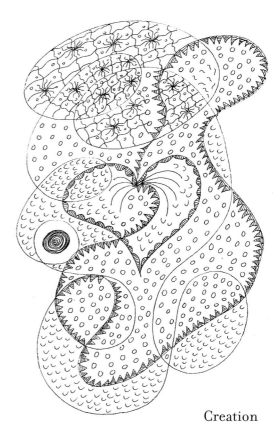

Creation

Tuy Nga Brignol, France
(birthplace: Vietnam)
INFLUENCE: SPIRITUALITY, CHANNELING,
MEDITATION, PRAYER

You Are Creation

(TRANSLATED FROM THE ORIGINAL FRENCH
BY THE POET)

Tuy Nga Brignol, France (birthplace: Vietnam)

INFLUENCE: SPIRITUALITY, CHANNELING,
MEDITATION, PRAYER

Everything in you asks only to take root
Everything in you is destined to grow
Do not choke anything in your heart
It is you yourself who creates your own
    Happiness
You did not come Here to copy
You came here to Create
In your own way
New experiences
You are Creation
As Is God

Light

Sara Manzotti, England

"It's always important to bring people together into a dimension of oneness. We're all spiritual beings. We all have the same source. And love is what binds us together, so we're all one universal family. The question we should ask ourselves is: 'what is my role in contributing to creating that universal family?' First, in order to bring peace to the world, I have to bring peace into my own soul. To bring love into the world, I have to actually feel, experience, and radiate it with authenticity. "

—REV. HOWARD E. CAESAR, USA

INFLUENCE: UNITY, UNIVERSAL SPIRITUAL TEACHINGS (ORIGINAL: LUTHERAN CHURCH)

Sutra Book

M. LaVora Perry, USA

INFLUENCE: BUDDHISM

"Whether you chant the Buddha's name, recite the sutra, or merely offer flowers and incense, all your virtuous acts will implant benefits and roots of goodness in your life."
—Nichiren, *On Attaining Buddhahood*

This little book,
covered in shiny black vinyl
with its gold-stamped crane
wearing off its front cover
is me.

I read these pages every day

Inside,
pages the color of mother's cream/
honey-hued after-milk,
fattening, rich spirit-food.
Right on top, in between, and all over
these white pages,
dance
all kinds of black-ink characters.

I read these pages every day

Words,
jump up off pages,
get me sucking space and air;
I am hungry to tell them to myself.

I read these pages every day

Turning pages,
I go deeper,
higher,
spreading wide
into my treasure house,
where hard, beautiful, rough-edged diamonds
dribble from my lips like precious juice.

I read these pages every day

I am dancing.
my heart
dances
my tongue
dances
my hips and mind
greedily snatch a selfless dance.
I weep sweet sweat—
gentle oil that readies me.

I read these pages every day

I pause,
kissing myself smiling,
knowing that when I sleep,
these urgent
centered
pages
are feeding me.

Asparagus May

Janet Baker, USA

INFLUENCE: SPIRITUALITY, YOGA, SHAMANISM, MEDITATION (ORIGINAL: ROMAN CATHOLICISM)

When I was little
I was so obsessed with war
I filled the garage with wounded sticks and twigs,
lined them up in rows,
and told my mother they were soldiers.

Asparagus, you are such sticks,
all the dying spears cut
before becoming ferns and berries.

I hold you like pencils,
write with you in fine calligraphy,
sprinkle blessings from your bundled tips.

Stubs of long fingers cut
every spring as you spear through earth,
your sentinels ascend,
sudden from surprised soil.

I trace your long shoots,
flick your chevron scales,
finer than fingernails in darkening pink.
I peel your satin green cover.

They sang to you in church,
chanted your name in long syllables,
for when they sang *asperges me*,
they really said asparagus may,
and when they sang *miserere mei*,
I sang for my own c.

On pilgrimage I carry you,
bouquet of cut asparagus.
A traveler said to take a bunch of ballpoint pens
to India for gifts and such.

At every mystery, I offer stalks of you instead,
and every guardian says you're good,
asparagus may, and lets me through.

Yellow Goat's Beard

John Knight, USA

INFLUENCE: SPIRITUALITY, NATURE, TRANSCENDENCE

The Whitening of the Ox:
A Circle Bending

K.V. Skene, England (birthplace: Canada)

INFLUENCE: SPIRITUALISM (ORIGINAL: ANGLICANISM)

The plum tree bows
to the wind. The sun drops too low
for daylight, too near
for sleep. I sit by a stream . . .

. . . water flows. Ox is all white.
Here, there is thick grass
for grazing, cool water for thirst,
songbirds to chase a stubborn soul
to sleep. I forget

when seasons turn, why birds fly south
who raised this sky, planted this earth,
how old I am. I remember
a dream repeating, a path
bending back on itself—a life
for a death and always a god
further on
just beyond where I am.

Depths of Light

Juliette Lagenour, USA

Butterfly House

Nancy Priff, USA

INFLUENCE: MEDITATION, PRAYER, MUSIC, ARTS (ORIGINAL: ROMAN CATHOLIC CHURCH)

This otherworld steams
jungle-hot, hushed and swollen
with wild Amazonian blooms.
Water washes over low flat stones.
The air pulses, flutters with life,
and I want to hold my breath,
be still as the windless flowers here,
and never disturb the fragile wings,
tendriled antennae, silent splendor.

But a storm of school children thunders in,
shouts shaking every frond. Oohs, aahs,
hands rise. Wild with desire, hungry
fingers snatch at the brilliant fliers.
A million graceful gliders transform—
gray-brown wings flatten into bark
and green ones form new leaves.
Others soar too high to see. So I wait,
watchful and silent as a prayer.

The teacher lectures on lepidoptera, boring
the beauty out of children's eyes. Soon,
they no longer notice the rainbow wings
of Urania, drifting down like a blessing,
or the blue-white Morpho twinkling
with the brightness of a falling star.
When the grade-school storm passes,
the butterfly house shakes itself
and takes a deep breath.

Then I feel the air
shift. Here and there,
wings open, rise, and stir the stillness.
On my arm, a Painted Lady lands
light as an angel's breath, an infant's soul.
She beats in streaks of sunset, gleaming
orange and black. Then the Lady pauses,
spreads her gauzy glory. Her dark feet,
barely touching, urge me to testify.

So I will be
the witness of wings.

Orchid Farms Fence and Post—Butterfly

Joel A. Schlauch, USA

INFLUENCE: ILLNESS, RECOVERY

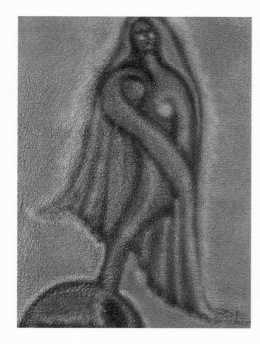

Madonna and Child

Ione Citrin, USA
INFLUENCE: JUDAISM

Golden

Kim Roberts, USA

In a break in the trees where the stream
winds through, they slant in, too ethereal
to be stripes, although there are two—

no, three—distinct beams shimmering,
    suspended in a honey mist.

I think of those religious paintings
of the Virgin ascending, or the saints
transformed by light at the exact moment
of their worst trial.

        Those beams are always wrong:
solid, sculptural, too heavy
to hang on air, or a different sort of dangerous:
like a crown of yellow knives.

        Not this porous curtain.
It appears and disappears. Against the slant of light,

the trees look gorgeous, greener, more themselves:
                the clarity of color,
the distinct outlines of individual leaves.

Although it's not light we see after all,
but bits of dust and dirt
            around which light coalesces.

Portraits of saints are poor representations
of the transfiguring moment.

    We only see what blocks
the light—the suspended matter—
the obstacles that glow with stubborn fire.

5
RITES AND RELIGION
The Significance of Doctrine, Rituals, and Practices

"My life is my practice."

—RAM DASS

Church

Marcus Antonius Jansen, USA

INFLUENCE: SPIRITUALITY

Almost a Buddhist

Lauren Crux, USA

INFLUENCE: SPIRITUAL QUESTIONING, IRONY

I'm almost a Buddhist, but that's like being a cat. You know how cats don't go completely out the door? You're standing there holding it open for them, and they walk halfway across the threshold, and stop. They just stand there, half in, half out. That's what I mean when I say I'm almost a Buddhist; I'm hanging out on the threshold.

A few years ago, I lived in a trailer park on the campus of the University of California at Irvine. It seemed that the entire campus was built on an anthill. I kept a clean kitchen, but if I left out even one crumb, there would be thousands of ants marching over the countertop. They were relentless. I tried everything: I dipped string in clove oil; used baking soda; I even tried talking to the ant queen, *Hey the guy next door is a slob, try him.*

But to no avail. They kept marching. And after a while, I just wanted to kill them. But this was a dilemma, because Buddhists are not supposed to kill. Then one day, I came across an article written by a Buddhist priest, who was having a similar problem. He had resolved it for himself and had come to a place of spiritual resolution. Just before he killed an ant, or any insect, he would say, *Better luck next time.*

"I started questioning the nature of the belief system that I was born into when I was about eleven or twelve. I am an only child and it was a harrowing time to have no one to talk to with all those questions in my head. It was extremely difficult because my parents told me I had to go to church with them. I found it meaningless and could not make a connection between ME and this God I was supposed to be worshipping. It made me feel very isolated and different."

—CECELIA ALPHONSUS, Malaysia

INFLUENCE: NEALE DONALD WALSCH, NATURE, WICCA, OTHERS (ORIGINAL: CATHOLICISM, BUDDHISM)

Buddha Diptych

Thomas Fuhs, USA
INFLUENCE: MULTIFAITH, DEVOUT YOGI

Ironic

Natalie N. Narine, USA
INFLUENCE: HINDUISM, NATURE (ORIGINAL: HINDUISM)

Growing up
Was it the dark skin or
What I was allowed to eat for lunch
I was the abscess on a cherry blossom tree
Called Hindu and hated fiercely
Keeping beliefs secret
Now it's trendy
Bindis to adorn superstar foreheads
Mehandi parlors as common as candy stores

Colorful saris and sarongs worn
By women of every creed
Nose rings just another body adornment
Sanskrit a fancy font
The food no longer stinky but delicacies
Gods and Goddesses on "regular clothing"
Temple a place to network like the Internet
Dissection to fit individual needs
A tree in everyone's yard.

Psalm for Another Sunday

SuzAnne C. Cole, USA

INFLUENCE: SPIRITUALITY

Holy Mother/Father God, I'm here again today
celebrating your creation in a Houston church,
wondering why I have come to this stone
    sanctuary—
    choir lofted fifty feet above and behind me
    raw brick walls, clashing colored glass,
    gilt and turquoise tile, spoon-shaped pulpit.
Do you dwell in the breasts of this proper flock
or with the homeless man I sped past earlier,
scribbled sign held high aloft:
                "I'm hungry
                I'm homeless
                I'm a vet
                God bless"?

Perhaps you inhabit the natural world
of today's mild March morning—
    wisteria decked in lavender majesty,
    redbud wearing passionate pink lace,
    azaleas shedding fast-fading blooms,
    arrogant-tailed mockingbird challenging
    a pair of mourning doves pacing boundaries—
cup of beauty freely offered, gratefully received.
Yet too thin this natural tonic;
too late to be a pantheist.

Today's sermon topic—
"Who needs religion?"
Holy Mother/Father God,
I guess that's why
I'm here again today.

Cooperation for Progress

Nereus Patrick Cheo, Cameroon

INFLUENCE: CATHOLICISM

You Are the Emollient

Jay Wilkinson, England

INFLUENCE: ISLAM (ORIGINAL: SPIRITUALISM, ISLAM [SUFISM, MYSTICS OF ISLAM])

You are the emollient that
Kept my heart soft
When working like a donkey made
My skin growl. I felt
Like an animal. Let down and
Wanting to be put
Down. I could not stand up I could
Only Look Down. Life
Was turbulent, mercenary
I was helplessly
Angry, my angry burns were soothed.
Shot through a canon
I sat wiping gunpowder off
My heavy shoulders
In front of you I exploded . . .
I am exploding
Still, you are busy soothing me.

I must be David
With these words my book of psalms and
This face my Bible.
Liberally petted in a
Rich emollient.
The cup no longer half empty.
Thirsty to drink.

It's a funny thing when the world
Puts you in a box
It soon represents a coffin.
No matter its lining:
To Be Alive Is to jump out.
Scare somebody with
Your eyes, your skin, your sin, your humility,
Mortality before God.
In front of you I exploded
From my tiny box.
Excitement still charges through me.
My head peaks, "Rab ig
Fir lee." Allah please forgive me
For: the years I feared
Being called a "Bloody woman,"
(…so expendable).

Seeing good people bleed.
(Just need time to heal.)
My eyes now the wound and the wound
Is so very vast.
You are The Emollient that
Keeps my heart soft.

*"I am Roman Catholic, but because I live in a multiethnic society,
I am open to other denominations and see the wisdom of some of these
teachings. We can all learn from each other."*

—SUELIN LOW CHEW TUNG, Grenada (birthplace: Trinidad)

INFLUENCE: ZEN BUDDHISM (ORIGINAL: ROMAN CATHOLICISM)

Opposite of Heaven

Joni Barker, USA

INFLUENCE: FRIENDS, FAMILY, CHRISTIAN IDEALS, NONDENOMINATIONAL CHURCH (ORIGINAL: PRESBYTERIANISM)

The man had already written HAPPY under HEAVEN and WORRY under HELL. I was going to Hell. If that wasn't bad enough, I was sure my mother was too because I had learned the art of worrying from her. It was part of my everyday life, and I didn't know how to function without it.

The instant I got home I searched my Bible for the passage that condemned me to Hell. I found only a few verses in the sixth chapter of Matthew that said not to worry because God will provide for you, there is no need to trouble yourself. That didn't satisfy my tormented mind; I searched and searched for the line that boldly declared, "Worry is a sin." I still haven't found it, which worries me a bit . . .

At that time, I had not yet learned to question the world around me. I don't remember when I began questioning the things I was told, but these experiences at church served to push me further away from religion.

I'm supposed to believe in God and Jesus, but beyond that, I never knew what was expected of me. My parents raised me to love and fear God, although I couldn't understood how to love someone (or something) I feared. By high school I had stopped attending church altogether, swearing that I could maintain a Christian lifestyle on my own. I planned to read the Bible and develop my own ideas instead of relying on others' interpretations. Instead, I ignored these promises I made to myself.

Perhaps the only thing that keeps me searching for a religion that suits me is the idea of Hell. I'm terrified of little devils with pitchforks, an eternity away from friends and family, and, of course, the scorching heat. I hate being hot.

Religion has always confused and worried me, so why do I feel the need to make room for it in my life? I must have a spiritual yearning I've failed to fulfill. I need to admit to myself that I believe in nothing. Besides, guilt fits into my life much easier than Sunday services.

*"I always wondered why religion divided people. And I wondered about God—
who's right here? Or has everybody got a piece of the truth? I wanted
to believe there's not just one group that's right; God is bigger than that. I felt
people should come together and not be separated by different denominations
of Christianity, world religions, or different philosophies or approaches.
There was the sense that the spirit was active in all,
the idea of 'one God many paths.'"*

—REV. HOWARD E. CAESAR, USA
INFLUENCE: UNITY, UNIVERSAL SPIRITUAL TEACHINGS (ORIGINAL: LUTHERAN CHURCH)

The Path
Donald Chandler, USA

*"Discovering the human nature of Jesus helped me have
a better understanding of Christianity, and opened my mind and spirit
to all manifestations of the Spirit as it is present in all religious traditions,
though always steeped in cultural influences to the point that it is sometimes
hardly recognizable. Therefore, I learned to pay attention to the good
that religions did for the people and the world, rather than the
bad things that people have done in the name of religion."*

—JAUME DE MARCOS, Spain
INFLUENCE: UNITARIAN UNIVERSALISM (ORIGINAL: CATHOLICISM)

A Religious Iconoclast's Melancholy Recollections of Childhood

Michael Meyerhofer, USA
INFLUENCE: ZEN BUDDHISM (ORIGINAL: ROMAN CATHOLICISM)

How would it have been for us
had they who taught the universe
every bleary Sunday morning
included with Hebrews and Acts
the lost Gospel of Thomas,
the death poetry of Zen monks,
Einstein's theory of relativity?

How would it have been to see
women in the same robes as men,
preaching philosophy alongside
those same fearful clichés of hell—
to know Jesus as olive-skinned
with hair like thick black thread,
a boy who suckled and liked it?

How would it have been to touch
the common chalice of our bodies
and feel without reproach the blood
roaring inside us like boiled wine,
to know God as wind and the atom,
to accept a universe that swells
and contracts like a beating heart?

How easy it would be to believe
that all our terrible doubts are born
from hearing only half the story,
that *they* in an inexcusable madness
rob or ignore what they cannot
understand—that if we had it all,

we'd actually be closer to home.

Double Buddha

Dmitri Poltavski, Russian Federation
INFLUENCE: ZEN BUDDHISM

The Ultimate Religious Retreat

Ivan G. Nassar, USA

INFLUENCE: ISLAM

"Labbayk, Allahumma. Labbayk. Labbayk. La shareeka laka. Labbayk.
Innal-hamda wan-n'imata laka wal-mulk. La shareeka lak." —Talbiyah

["Here we come, O Allah, here we come! Here we come. No equals do You have.
Here we come! Truly the praise and blessings are yours—the Kingdom too! No
equals do You have."]

This monotonous chorus reverberated like sound waves floating on the currents
of human emotions as the message of Islam transcended the many dialects of the
throng of worshippers beginning their journey of a lifetime: the Pilgrimage to Mecca
or simply, the Hajj.

In the last month of the Islamic lunar calendar, Zu'l Hijjah, I was blessed to be in
the company of pilgrims from around the world in the hot desert country of Saudi Ara-
bia, including over five hundred worshippers from my American Muslim community.

Feeling as if I had a crown of precious jewels on my head, I was ready for the
pinnacle of my spiritual preparation and financial sacrifices.

Once inside the compound of the Grand Mosque, I joined the swelling ranks
making their circumambulation around the Ka'aba. I found myself swooped up in this
evolving human wheel, individualism quickly squashed beneath its driving force.
The energy emanating from this counterclockwise movement produced a tidal wave
of emotions that intensified the spiritual experience. Day and night a steady stream of
pilgrims entered the confines of the sacred Mosque to perform this ritual.

On the ninth day of Zu'l Hijjah, pilgrims journey to Mount Arafat to participate
in the most important ceremony of the Hajj. The multitude marches before their Lord,
bringing their personal grief in spiritual obedience, with the hope of evolving into a
state of spiritual excellence. The Prophet has stated: "He who performs the Hajj with
no obscenity or evil will come out as a newborn baby free from all sins; there is no
reward . . . except the reward of paradise." As if suspended in a heavenly dimension
somewhere between life and death, the pilgrims engage in the ritual of prayer from
noon until sunset.

At sundown, a fellow Muslim retrieved a bottle of water from his backpack; the
water refreshed our tired bodies and the experience of Mount Arafat enriched our
souls, our worldly cares evaporating into the sands of the desert landscape.

Soul Searcher

Tobias Beharrell, Canada
INFLUENCE: TRUST IN A
GREATER PLAN/POWER
(ORIGINAL: LITTLE TO NONE)

The Retreat

Janet McCann, USA

Signing up
She's maybe seventy, solid built,
accents of Ireland.
Sister Mary of course.

I say, *it's sad
there are no more postulants*
(this left the rooms free
for us) but she
says *No,*

*what is old has to pass
away in the Church,
we serve the Lord
differently now
and when we nuns are
gone, our work will still
be there, invisible in the
world.*

Later she leads us out
to the roof to teach us Tai Chi.
Sturdy and graceful,
she balances
near the roof's edge,

her dark swathed arms
like wings.

Black Math

Harold L. Hoffman, USA

INFLUENCE: ZEN BUDDHISM, HINDUISM, CHRISTIANITY (ORIGINAL: BAPTIST CHRISTIANITY, AGNOSTICISM)

For David

I

tell me it was something valuable,
a jazzman's trumpet,
a ballplayer's bat,
a blindman's dog.
not a Honda Civic
or an unfinished armoire.

grand theft seems so paltry.
it makes me hope
your cell feels like a womb
wallpapered with razor wire.

everywhere here seems crowded
with cacti. staring into the desert,
on my second cup of coffee,
i've spent the morning performing
calculations, drying up,
thirty-two miles from home.

how many years,
months, days will it take
before you're free?

i hate math.
two hours after lunch,
every day,
in the fourth grade.
same problems,
different numbers:

i knew every solution
without flipping to book's end
but never could show my work
and nobody believed me.

if i only knew,
i might have toiled
like a Spartan

or given up sooner,
realizing education is just
a battle of attrition.

II

dressed up like candy, she slithers
across frayed linoleum.
for a moment, i think
i've stepped into
someone else's fetish.

i ask for a pen
but i want her
to talk dirty, lean hard
on the counter, bare
her cherry bra. instead,
she fills my cup
puts a ballpoint down,
asks politely that i not steal it.

i write: *brother, i've been told
that you found Jesus
in prison. that's great . . .*
who am i kidding?
i folded the napkin twice,
put it in the nether regions
of my coat pocket.

everyone is finding Jesus.
he's at the local Cineplex.
it's his second coming
since nobody reads
or trusts their own
imagination anymore.

i should have crucified you
years ago. watching you fade
behind piles of antique dentistry
equipment, psychedelic Fillmore
posters, ten-inch records.

forgive me. i didn't know
what you were looking for.

III

it's all gone now.
you have Jesus
and Kali has found me.

rubbing my nape,
she looks for the spot
to drive her sword,
give me a soldier's death.

instead, she uses the countertop
as a sheaf. a slain demon's head
finds my empty soup bowl.

in spite of the blood
on her breasts,
she looks hungry.

i flag the waitress
but she refuses to serve us.
no shirt, no shoes, no service.

i guess a girdle of dead
men's hands and a necklace
of fifty skulls isn't enough.

nothing's ever enough.

IV

responsibility never blossomed
in the garden under your scalp.
that's what mom and dad thought.

still, the slot-car track
they raced each day
rarely changed despite

the ceaseless work
done by men in orange vests.

pocketing the waitress' pen,
i brave the mid-morning
with my goddess of destruction.

her skin shimmers onyx.
the street's colors dissolve
in her four arms' embrace.
i love this city.
there is such desperation here,
she says, her red tongue whipping.

i miss you, i admit.

i've missed your misery most, she says.
how you moved like a juggernaut.

walking away, she leaves
bloody footprints.

V

my futility has always been supported
by Newton's Second Law of Motion.

with no force,
mass is sedentary.
i didn't want to believe this
when i was sixteen.

disgusted with time and space,
i tried to slice through the cosmos
with a hatchet-mind. that night
on our dinner table
carbon bled from pencils,
marring anything white
with imperfections.

when the sun rose my eyes

were packed with eraser dust.
i blinked and found myself
at the foot of a paper-thin mountain
of disappointment that festered
through the night.

memories of you banged
on the shower door and cursed
while i watched water disappear
into the drain, wondering if
gravity is just having no place
else to go. these thoughts snapped
by chattering teeth.

lost in the Universe at large.
i rode the bus to school
then straight through town.

cars slingshotted through streets.
children pinballed in playgrounds.
the Galaxy stirred. my thoughts,
grains of sand in a blender.
i needed to stop and pulled the bell.

VI

the problem with physics
is black and white stand in
for a tapestry of grays.

whole theories are Holland dikes,
riddled with imperfections,
holding back oceans of doubt.
while everyone ignores
the creaks, gazing back
and stumbling over the headstones
of those they're superseding.

i couldn't show my work
but i've known the whole time.
the answer to every question
is the same
and when we don't believe
the solution, we create
Gods, Goddesses, and servants.

once, there was only sunrise
and sunset. we created years,
months, days, and hours,

so everyone would show up
to the same place,
at the same moment,
drop to their knees,
and bow in unison.

but anything created
or believed
will bind us,
appointments and passions
the worst thistles on brow,
nails through palms.

just wait, in 2,090 days
you'll simply move
from one cell to another.

sleep well brother.
sleep well.

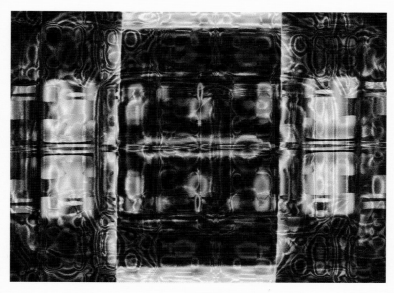

Temple

Virginia C. Fairchild, USA

INFLUENCE: SPIRITUALITY

*"I was confused as to why I belonged to my religion and culture by birth,
yet people couldn't relate to me because I looked different.
The more I thought about it, the more questions kept erupting. My culture,
the religion I inherited, the history of it all. Endless questions . . .*

*"I was traveling a lot and liked to talk to new people. In the midst
of my material life, I started seeing some answers because I could see other
points of view. Deep down we are all the same, it's just how we grow up
and our exposure to life. I am not ready to say that I found the answers to
my questions, but somewhere I am hitting at a matrix of hints here and there.
And I am still being led to those answers whenever I open myself and
let others share their part and perspective of life."*

—THANGJAM RANJAN SINGH, India

"African religion incorporates the dead and Christianity tells us to forget them. I hovered between the two worlds successfully until my mother died. Now I find that my soul lacks a home."

—SIBUSISIWE NKOMO, USA (birthplace: Zimbabwe)
INFLUENCE: SKEPTICISM (ORIGINAL: CHRISTIANITY)

Finding My Religion

Brian Eule, USA

One of my best friends thinks I am going to hell.

It's never mentioned and, to tell the truth, I rarely think about it. It has nothing to do with our friendship, nor with why he is a religious man.

When I came to college, I was not sure of my religious beliefs. I knew I was Jewish, that my mother followed lots of religious rules that I thought made no sense, and that she expected me to do the same. What I didn't know was what I thought about God. I didn't want to say that God didn't exist, for fear he did, but I struggled to believe entirely.

My Christian roommate not only believed; he knew. I learned how much religion and spirituality meant to him and greatly appreciated that he never pushed his beliefs on me. Instead, he led by example. I got to see how his faith made him a better person.

I envied this faith. As a result, I searched for my own, looked for answers and found some, something I probably wouldn't have done so early in my life had I not met him. God became part of my life, too, even though I still did not follow many of the rules of my religion. Rules foster a relationship, I decided, and to let religious rules be the sole guiding force of my spirituality was to let the cart drive the horse. Instead, I wanted to let my new relationship with God be enhanced by those religious rules that helped the relationship. Judaism began to mean something to me. Some of the rules served this purpose, and those I followed. Others I ignored.

Crossing the Street

Rita Ogburn-McCall, USA
INFLUENCE: SPIRITUALITY, CHRISTIANITY

Crossing the street
I noticed a bag woman
at the corner and pitied her.
She needs to be saved.

A smile spread her lips

in my direction.
I too smiled in ignorance
at those who passed me,
but now I know better.
She stared at the crease
I left in my shift. The iron took too long
to heat and I was in a hurry.
Some people have no understanding.
They need to be saved.

A block ahead, a man tipped his hat
to me. He looked like the men
who would hold out dollar bills
and laugh as I tried to plead
my young way into access.
So I turned my head,
he needs to be saved.
A woman stumbled past me
pulling close her purse. Her two-inch
heel caught my toe, we collided.
The odor of her cologne embraced me.

It was 1983, the club was jumpin'
Mick Daniels was rubbing
on my butt. My halter hung low
with sweat over heartbeats
deep as base controlling
the crowd. I lost his baby
and him the same night.
So here is this woman apologizing for her life.
That girl needs to be saved.

A couple blocked my way
into the corner store. He smiled
into her eyes and she into his;
just like Thomas and me
before I found out he was married.
His wife called my house
every day looking for him
until I realized that I wasn't the only
other one and told her so.
And we cried and
she got saved.
I pushed my way past
these two, who showed no compassion
for others. So absorbed in lust
and emptiness. Caught up in each other,
they looked through me, around me.
I take much care to be removed now.
Since Sister Lucy sat me down
at Holy Gospel Rebellion and said
the red stockings made Henry beat me.
Short skirts made Julius take me
from my mother's home to lose me.
The cut of my blouse brought tears
to the eyes of women. Too much lipstick
and eyeliner made Jesus not love me.
She gave me a plain brown wrapper
and a scowl to wear
—then I was saved,
then I was saved.

"My maternal grandfather passed away when I was twelve. He was my best friend, mentor, and teacher rolled all into one, so his death was difficult. It was made more difficult by the behavior of an aunt who was part of a church run by a televangelist. According to her beliefs, since her father had not attended church in ten years, he was destined to go to Hell. (It didn't seem to matter that he was bedridden with emphysema, or that he had a local minister making house calls.) Very upset and angry, I made the decision that if Grandpa was going to be in Hell, I'd rather go there than spend eternity without getting to see him again, and that was the beginning of a great questioning."

—REV. TAMARA SIUDA, USA

INFLUENCE: KEMETIC ORTHODOXY (ORIGINAL: UNITED METHODIST CHRISTIANITY)

St. Paul

Oleg Korolev, Ukraine (birthplace: Russia)

INFLUENCE: ORTHODOX CHRISTIANITY HESYCHASM (ORIGINAL: ART)

Sacraments

Lisa M. Kelley, USA

INFLUENCE: PERSONAL SPIRITUAL QUEST (ORIGINAL: CATHOLICISM)

BAPTISM

Birth of a brother
and we walk to church
where we will,
my mother tells me,
give him to God.
When we get home I wipe the
oil from his forehead.

He is mine.

COMMUNION

Sunday Mass
with Grandpa.
Genuflect
and sit with him
listen to him ask the priest
How the hell are you, Father?
in delight and shock.
body and blood
Wonder what he confesses
when he disappears behind the curtain.
Sit with him
in the glow of red and blue glass.

I have his wooden rosary beads
(Peace be with him)
in a case
(and with me)
on my dresser
(forgive me).

CONFIRMATION

I do not find
as my mother did
years before,
what I do not have
at home.
I look for
what I am missing
but it is not here.

I declare myself
claim a new name
and move on.

RECONCILIATION

I believe Jesus
but God is too abstract
for me
to hold on
I do not go to church
but Sundays with Grandpa
live in me
I try
but

Bless me father
for I sin repeatedly
make the same mistakes
want to call you mother too
Demand explanations
try to be grateful
try
bless me.

What Sunday Has Become to Me

V. William Barrett, USA

INFLUENCE: ECCLESIASTICAL POETRY (ORIGINAL: LATTER-DAY SAINTS [MORMONISM])

Growing up in a Latter-Day Saints family and environment, which was often spiritually fulfilling, left me hungry for an outside world, that is, of the artistic milieu gaining popularity at that time: avant-garde art, experimental film, and especially rock, such as the late 1960s Beatles and Pink Floyd. In Church I was warned of the dangers of these kinds of influences, but I was not sure why they were evil, and I'm still not sure why today. I do now recognize the inherent dangers of drug abuse that often accompanied the life of a liberal artist or rock musician, but I only learned that lesson myself through hard, rough paths without roadmaps, never via a Sunday school lesson.

My own background in religion is a little like a winding mountain road that only very rarely straightens out—and then for very short distances. Restful Sundays, perhaps reading scripture, perhaps a poem, is what religion has become to me.

DO NOT CONSIDER THE FACTS AS THEY ARE: GO ACCORDING TO YOUR INNER CONVICTIONS.

Truth Goodness and Beauty 5

Doug McGoldrick, USA

INFLUENCE: BUDDHISM (ORIGINAL: CATHOLICISM)

This Old Dress I Call Jewish

Robin Greene, USA
INFLUENCE: BUDDHISM (ORIGINAL: JUDAISM)

This dress in my closet has been
here since my birth—every year
I look at it, press it to my body
before a full-length mirror and see
a thick-waisted peasant woman
walk the dirt road to market.

Once, its color blazed vermillion,
like heat or anger, but now the dress
has faded to ochre, the color of dried
blood—and time has loosened
its pleats like ocean waves
that mourn a sinking ship.

Every year I take it from my closet,
watch it come alive again, drop
from its wooden hanger in a strange
submissive grace as I bend to hear
its cries and muttered prayers,
my face to its zipper, smelling its stale
breath, feeling its rib cage heave.

Almost a century ago, my grandparents
came from Russia with this dress,
crossed Europe, the Atlantic, and arrived
at Ellis Island. All the women
in my family have worn it.

But listen—you have to understand—
I try to be good, do what's right.
But this dress has never fit nor given me
solace—it hangs in my closet like the guilt
I won't wear, an obligation I can't embrace.

Christmas Quest

Ed Calhoon, USA

INFLUENCE: ROMAN CATHOLICISM, ECUMENICAL CHRISTIANITY
(ORIGINAL: PRESBYTERIANISM, EVANGELICAL PROTESTANTISM)

Literary criticism
was the Grinch
that stole Christmas,
as a result of an
incomplete seminary education.

The problem was not
disbelieving Santa and his elves,
but throwing out
the Baby Jesus
with the proverbial textual bathwater.

Scholars much smarter than me
(like the later Jesus Seminar)
were the source of my skepticism,
with their search, like Schweitzer,
in Quest of the Historical Jesus.

They try to pick out *pericopes*,
authentic nuggets of true text
mined from the ore of myth.
The danger is losing faith
in the discarded slag heap of scripture.

After leaving seminary,
I wandered in the spiritual desert.
Then I read in *Roots*
about the author meeting a *griot*
in the African homeland of his ancestors.

He was a storyteller with
hundreds of years
of memorized narratives
encompassing the history
of his people in poetic form.

He demonstrated the ability
of otherwise illiterate people
to accurately pass on
verbal traditions
through the centuries.

Later in my pilgrimage,
I read Cardinal Newman's *Apologia*,
in which he told of his
discovery of the continuity
of verbal and written tradition.

Tradition linked the apostles
and the early Church Fathers
leading to the Councils
that created the Canon of Scripture
and wrote the Creeds of the Church.

The living church and its message
created the Scripture,
not vice versa
(per the Protestant creed:
Sola Scriptura).

After becoming Catholic,
I completed the Spiritual Exercises
Of Saint Ignatius Loyola
using my limited imagination
to place myself in the Gospel stories.

My spiritual director was a Jesuit
Biblical scholar
who showed me it was possible
to do scriptural analysis
without discarding tradition.

He also showed an openness
to the new winds of the Spirit
blowing in the Charismatic movement,
which many other denominations
had been unable to accept and cast out.

I remembered a young sailor I met
in Vietnam who was one of
the first Catholic Charismatics
and was a beacon of light
in an otherwise dark situation.

I found that the Church
had adapted to the challenges
of each generation.
Saint Ignatius was part of
the Counter-Reformation.

Ignatius used many of the
terms of evangelical Protestantism
and even showed Charismatic gifts,
enough to be hauled before
the Inquisition under suspicion.

The Spirit that inspired the Scriptures
still speaks to the Church
in the new Millennium,
and as many Christmases
as are left to come.

Fatima

Ana Maria Marques, Portugal

6
DIVINE DISCOURSE
Shaping Spiritual Beliefs through Prayer, Meditation, and Communion with Divinity

"The happiest man is he who learns from nature the lesson of worship."

—RALPH WALDO EMERSON

Turning the Beads

ShantiMayi, France
INFLUENCE: INDIGENOUS WISDOM, EASTERN RELIGION,
CHRISTIANITY (ORIGINAL: RUSSIAN ORTHODOX CHURCH)

Candles

Ana Maria Marques, Portugal

Lighting a Candle for My Mother and Father at Chartres Cathedral

Thom Tammaro, USA

INFLUENCE: ROMAN CATHOLICISM

"And yet there is someone, whose hands infinitely calm, hold up this falling."
—Rainer Maria Rilke

If you were here, you would do the same for me: drop a coin in the metal offering box, light your candle with the flame from another, then offer me a prayer. But who receives the prayer of the doubter? Perhaps this wall, thick and blackened with the soot and smoke of candles for a hundred years? Or is this where grief and sorrow go when they leave the hearts of the ones for whom the candles were lit?

Sometimes, walking home at dusk, I'll notice a light going on in the room of a house along the street where I live now and remember the child from those awkward years when he was lost in the world. How, climbing the hill toward home, he would steady his body against the cold, fix his eyes on the light in the window, and pray he would not die before reaching the only place he ever wanted to be.

The architect designs a space where we can find our way through the labyrinth of grief to the holy place. Your light was the gift I followed. Today, lighting this candle, I whisper your names.

Elegy Otherness

J. D. Smith, USA

INFLUENCE: CHRISTIANITY, BUDDHISM (ORIGINAL: EASTERN & WESTERN CHRISTIANITY)

What really is there to do, then?
What is there, really, to do?
The day demands its repetitions:
to eat with bowls and spoons
that have been washed before
and will need to be washed again;
to eliminate, to bathe
with a melting bar of soap,
allegory of the flesh
it foams across;
to take in water and refresh
the body's stem
in its fragile vase of years.

Still, between parentheses of sleep
remain hours that must be filled
with jobs, and loves, and other pastimes
to stave off boredom
and the thought of death.

When they do, we are left
with a surplus consciousness,
given as the grass,
that could not have helped
distant ancestors to hunt or mate,
but confronted them as if
a weather or terrain had
extended into the mind
and, like any harsh land,
made them perish quickly, or adapt.

Adapting still, we try to grasp
an Otherness that will not go away
but infuses things, rests behind,
or joins them, and resists
our efforts to excise or ignore it;
one could more readily tear away
a piece of cloud
and keep it in an open hand.
Instead, we can only
draw near that Presence,
and among those who approach
as well, find warmth.

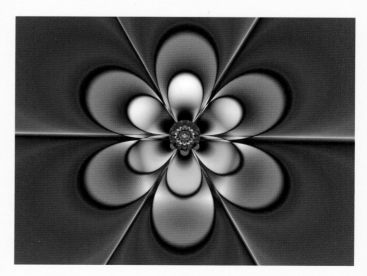

Shining Lotus

Virginia C. Fairchild, USA
INFLUENCE: SPIRITUALITY

Prayer

John M. FitzGerald, USA

INFLUENCE: SACRED WRITINGS, GOD'S INFLUENCE

Now, I stare into emptiness,
Alone enough for poetry;
Alone enough for even me;
Alone requiring mention of time.
There are these words, and sounds,
An order, tone, evasive emotions
I've known so long, just not acknowledged;
But others begin to notice frozen souls.
I don't know why I seem surprised at life,
I'm making it happen, I let it run wild.
I ought to rein it in a little,
Maybe do some real work.
Give me that alpha rhythmic vibe,
And I'll go one-on-one with God.
God is not too busy for people like me;
I say, you are no God without me.

You are words, to be written,
And I am here now.
Just stay there being nothing
Like a cipher, irreducible,
While I describe the sound
As a question worthy of presupposing
How it comes and goes.
Do you want to see it again?
You are a story with no facts,
A line at a time;
I don't even notice you go,
You return so fast.
You are a lonely aging man
Who calls a grandchild
And wonders when he's coming back.
I'm like that too, not needing to believe.

Breath

Suzanne Fossey, England

Streetcar

John McKernan, USA
INFLUENCE: CATHOLICISM

      What was the nun's name? She was younger
than all the other sisters Taller Thinner
Her nun outfit lined and curlicued

      constantly with board chalks of many colors
It's her perfumes I remember most
The threads of skin cream and hand soap Hints

      of shampoo Soft sneezy puffs of chalk
Brilliant the geographical oranges
of the Florida map The polished beads

      and cross on Oh Yes! Sister Mary
Adam's seemingly infinite jute-string
redwood cross and carved bead rosary

      Our screams deep within our eyes
itching in parkas and wool caps Sister
held us there stunned to stitched mouths

      A single finger to her pink chapped lips
brushing now Angela Pattavina's
long black hair ending her lecture on prayer

      with these final words "You can pray all the time
No one on earth needs to know you're praying
You don't need a church You might just be sitting

      on the wicker seat of a streetcar staring
at the garbage and beauty of the world Sunset
or car wreck We can fill our brains with some

      thing else than the junk of the world Candy
wrappers and broken kite string" I shook my head
Those words at that moment seemed the strangest

      sounds from the world I had ever heard I
kept repeating that day the word *streetcar*
so many times its meaning dissolved

      as a child's cry or a pink cloud will dis-
appear in a sky at twilight or a grain
of sugar melt in a bead of ice water

Clean

Marcus Antonius Jansen, USA
INFLUENCE: SPIRITUALITY

Angel

Olukunle Ayodeji Ogundele, Nigeria

INFLUENCE: CHRISTIANITY, NATURE

I may not be able to see you
But I know you are here
In my deep silence I feel you
In my troubled mind I hear your voice
Calming all the stormy wave
You may not know how pain is
But you felt mine
You guide in my thought telling me things to do
Still, free will is what you teach
Your presence always brings peace
Sailing over my deep emotion
I don't have to see you
    But your presence is what I crave

Enlightenment

Elisha Miller, USA

INFLUENCE: SPIRITUALITY, METAPHYSICAL ART

Inner Silence

Peter Corbett, England

INFLUENCE: MEDITATION

The thoughts do not arise.
The sea is calm.
The way is clear as crystal.
It is the realm of bliss and light.
It achieves no end but itself;
Self-imposed and self-serving.
It is the beacon that beckons us all,
But few follow.
It is the center of the maze,
And the place of no-name:
The experience beyond heaven and hell—
The inner silence of the magical wind.

Logos

Ruth Calder Murphy, England

What is this life?
Mists swirl hypnotic
in the desert.
A mirage beckons,
shimmers and dies as I must.
In the internal winter
I feel the heat of exposure
to its glacial heart
and then the mists return and so do I.
In the labyrinthine caverns
I see the light of
death's quick blade.
In the primal moon
of my inner eye
I see your light reflected.
Turning the chaotic seasons of my sphere to order,
you rise to bring meaning into life.

Claws of the Moon

Durlabh Singh, United Kingdom (India, Kenya)
INFLUENCE: SIKHISM (ORIGINAL: INDIAN METAPHYSICS)

Retreat Song, the Stuff of Life

Kathryn Gessner, USA

INFLUENCE: TIBETAN BUDDHISM

I wake in the morning to the residue of a dream about shoes. Matching them to the right outfit. I am alone in a sparse cabin in southern Oregon, a temporary forest dwelling. I have a denim duffel full of the worst of my shorts and T-shirts. When I get dressed, I will match the colors properly. No one is here to see me.

A dream about fashion shows me my mind. I could say I dreamed about catching the next insight, the contemporary edge on Buddhist philosophy, the best new daycare system, or any other sometimes-great domestic notion. But I dreamed about Mary Janes—here in the great Pacific Northwest, in a woodland cabin, a long way from the nearest skirt, I chose the Reiker Mary Jane shoes, leather, black, with a small heel, to match the outfit for the day, and then I awoke, rolled out of bed to Tevas and a pair of worn-out shorts. . . .

The sun meets the empty floor, and there is some warmth. I slide into its rays and sit there on a blanket and meditation cushion. I am "on retreat." Retreat is where you go to find enlightenment, a peaceful mountain cabin or a cave, a hole carved in rock. You take your candles and your *mala*, a little rice. It doesn't matter if you have a home, a career, a past. Here is the retreat cabin, a plain futon, sheets you brought from home, and the whole day stretches ahead of you as the sun moves across the floor. Outside, poison oak awaits you on the walk to the communal kitchen. And I dreamed about Mary Janes in black leather with a small heel. I'm guessing enlightenment is a long way off.

I breathe and settle into a half-lotus. Nothing much is happening. I won't shave my armpits or legs or even brush my hair. No deodorant, no suffering, no origination, no stopping, no path, no cognition, but some Kotex is really helpful. I also brush my teeth, ritually. The American Dental Association recommends tooth brushing, flossing, checkups every six months. Drill and fill with poisonous substances in new tooth-colored products attached with some bonding agent to the bone.

My mind this morning settles on how artificial this idea of retreat can be, how selfish, another accumulation of stuff. I mean, shouldn't I give up brushing my teeth, too? I rise from the cushion, get my toothbrush, walk outside to the bathroom, up the step, into the sink area, sloshing soap and warm water, heated water! What a luxury! I glance there in the mirror. Steady glance at my face.

The famous yogis of the past have achieved enlightenment without brushing their teeth. In the echoing silence of the water sucking down the drain, I begin to hear the woods stir, the songbirds, the crows. I am not alone here, although no other humans are around.

Retreat is not exciting. Peak experiences here mean you've gone nuts. Like a dream, the day condenses years as thoughts pass like a flash of lightning, illuminating the person I once was. I seem to be someone else, housed in a similar body, sitting on a cushion warmed by the sun filtering through tree branches. I become much like the furniture in the room, since there is none, and the room itself is neither here nor there. Hours pass like this. Reverentially. It's not exactly like the poem, but Emily Dickinson comes to mind: *I heard a fly buzz when I died*. On days like this, I think of her. But she wore brown shoes.

It's time for lunch, I can tell. I feel that aching longing beneath the ribs, and I am stiff and cold from sitting. I don't even like Emily Dickinson all that much. Why would I want to imitate her life? My mind is back to work. Toothbrushing and Emily Dickinson and Kotex—what do they have in common?

Untitled

Tomas Kapocius, Lithuania
INFLUENCE: ROMAN CATHOLICISM

The Single Prayer

Eve Jackson, Isle of Wight, England

INFLUENCE: QUAKERISM

To those far away
strangers I shall never meet,
I wrap my thoughts in a prayer.

Cradled between solemn promises
and wishful dreams
are Words of Peace.

My single prayer, a lingua franca
amidst a chorus of new mornings
everywhere.

Layers of hope, doubt,
hope, may fall away
like tiny distractions,

but in reaching out
strands of love will unravel,
from hand to helping hand, heart

to mind. Drawing the circle
ever closer. The space between
changing, as the act of unwrapping

re-shapes every one of us,
until Peace is born
of us all.

Synagogue Series #5

Kevin Katz, USA

INFLUENCE: REFORM JUDAISM (ORIGINAL: JUDAISM)

TeleJombo

Tirzo Martha, Netherlands Antilles

Luce

Jon Marie Broz, USA

INFLUENCE: MULTIFAITH SPIRITUALITY

I would pray for strength.
Pray for a sign.
Lighting candles while kneeling stiff, on chilled risers
of rosso, crema, serpentine.
Dropping coins in the lead-lipped offering box,
I bought sticks of balsam
to set fire to my pleadings.
Beseeching leather-winged angels,
as flaming waxes in jewel-colored glass,
dipped and rose, clustered in the dim.
I seethed with lack of vision,
clouded from lack of clarity,
breathed, from the corners of my mouth.

I was caught, a snake eating its tail
in some pagan myth,
a mobius of unanswered prayers,
extinguished: I had gone out.
Then fueled by your hope,
the burning curled back the darkness,
to reveal unearthly light.
Life blew in;
blew in, dipping and rising,
blew in, over the flaming waxes,
clustered in the dim.

Can I Be Here in the Emptiness?

Vince Gowmon, Canada

INFLUENCE: SPIRITUAL ENLIGHTENMENT

(ORIGINAL: AGNOSTICISM)

Can I be here in the emptiness?

Where the heart is open
And the mind is clear
The body wants nothing
And I'm open to hear
A sound in the wind
A brush of a tree
The storm of the night
The voice beyond the dream

Can I be here in the emptiness?

Where over the days
And over the years
It's been calling to me
Beyond my fears
Come back to this moment
Come back right now
Come back from your dream
It's here life is found

Can I be here in the emptiness?

Where I stop searching
And finally let go
Of all my ambitions
And all I think I know
Of what I've sought after
And what I thought true
Of everything I am
And everything I do
There's nothing more
For me here now
There's nothing left to seek
All around

Can I be here in the emptiness?

Leaving the dream
Is all I've had to do
To let go of it all
And remember my truth

I am nothing more
Than endless love
An infinite speck
Of timeless love
A drop of water
In a pool of light
A powerful presence
That shines so bright

The gift of God
Is for me to know
There's nothing to do
And nowhere to go
It's all in my heart
Just let it come through
My light, my joy
The love that's my truth

Can I be here in the emptiness?

Meditation (Tribute to Shri Dhyanyogi)

Chris Dei, USA

INFLUENCE: STATE OF SAMADHI

Dr. Joe Lindley

USA, philosopher, healer, musician, and teacher

INFLUENCE: ONE AND ALL (ORIGINAL: CHRISTIANITY)

Was there a time when you questioned the nature of spirit and how to incorporate it into your life?

I do not remember a time when I didn't question the nature of spirit; it has always been in the forefront of my thought. Spirituality has always been my "self righting mechanism" that keeps me on course. I have seriously thought many times during my life about becoming a monk and devoting my entire life to the pursuit of spiritual awareness. Instead, I have chosen to apply this same pursuit to any and all areas of my life and still function in the world. In essence I have become an "urban monk."

What were the major questions you were dealing with?

I was living in a state of mystery, questioning what even the questions should be. It was not so much a questioning but rather a deep curiosity or yearning . . . I never consciously asked the basic questions—why am I here? what is our purpose? who am I? where did I come from?—but I have always received an awareness related to them. I do frequently ponder what God is, how I can get closer to this source I'm irresistibly attracted to, and the difference between life and death and the space before or after. My spirituality is in a completely different realm than the conscious, based more on intent than questions.

Please describe your personal experience of those questions.

Questions or intent, in my case, are seeds. Once asked and pondered, they grow, whether I think them consciously or not. But questions of this nature do not necessarily have finite answers and frequently lead to more and deeper questions. I find that the intent for answers is always just below the conscious level. I have a sense that answers will be revealed at the right time, when I can understand them, and I enjoy the wait. It has been during these waiting periods that my trust in God has been developed.

What was it like to realize you might be able to resolve these questions for yourself?

"Resolve" may not apply in my case—it is more the satisfaction of learning to love the mystery of it all. I think the more you ask, are curious, or have your intent directed toward knowing, the more is revealed. I do not feel that I am necessarily going to resolve all questions, but that is now okay. The questions and answers just make the personal universe get bigger and bigger. The bigger it gets, the more mystery there is. "Mystery" is my only accurate definition of the spiritual path and the God it leads to.

Why follow a spiritual path of any kind (as opposed to a particular path)?

First, I think it is important to mention that there are many different degrees of spiritual paths. These range from living a "normal" existence "accessorized" by spiritual thought and ritual, to living in a state of constant prayer, awareness, and devotion to God. For those in the first group, spirituality colors their path, gives it meaning, and ultimately may reshape or redefine their personal path. The people I know on the other extreme live in a constant state of prayer or meditation and literally "live to pray" rather than "pray to live." Those in the first group go about their normal lives and try to add some spiritual spices into the mix. Those in the second have jobs and careers, mainly for survival, and their work is dedicated to a higher good, or they may have devoted their entire lives to monastic duties.

With that said, I think the importance of following a spiritual path is ultimately to connect us to the ONE, to make us aware that we are all ONE and from the same source. To be connected to this truth is very powerful. You cannot be connected to the ONE and inflict pain or suffering on another human being or the planet or any sentient being for that matter, because you are inflicting it on yourself. We are Godlike, individual extensions of the one source, but we have not recognized that quality and power yet. We have not fully developed into what we can become. When we do, this life and this world will be a different and far better place. We will approach "Heaven on Earth."

Do you identify primarily with one spiritual group, and is this the one you were introduced to as a child?

I identify, to some degree, with all spiritual groups. I was raised in Christianity but have explored on my own Buddhism, Taoism, and many other religions since age eight or so. I am fascinated with cultures in general as well as the religions that sprang from them. I am interested in their spiritual practices, prayers, and meditations, but most interested in their final product and whether they bring humanity toward the ONE or create division. I feel very satisfied when religion and true spirituality coexist but find it rather rare. I am appalled by dogma. I appreciate all attempts to celebrate God and am amused at almost all attempts to define an indefinable God. Remembering that Jesus was not a Christian and Buddha not a Buddhist, I try to decipher the true essence of these and all spiritual teachings. So to answer the question, I keep returning to the teachings of Jesus, those of peace, love, and compassion for our fellow man. I look to the teachings of Buddha for the ethics of daily living. And to Taoism for its wisdom, practicality, and explaining the unexplainable. I identify with the truth I have found along my path.

Call Me Miriam's Daughter

Joanne Seltzer, USA

God, I don't pretend to see your face
or hear your voice or touch your flowing robes
or smell your essences or taste
hypnotic embers of eternal fire
that came to Moses as a lump of coal,

all I want, God, is the assurance
you're there for me whenever I cry out.

In return, I offer you my face,
my voice, my flowing dress, my essences,
my passionate response to this domain
only Neanderthals consider flat.

Teach me how to grow through womansong,
how to die with dignity and strength,
how to keep endangered sparks alive.

Eyes

Paulette Sharron Stewart, New Zealand

My Grandmother Prays

Veneta Masson, USA

INFLUENCE: HEALING ART

It bothered my brother
that she whispered her
nightly prayers
loud enough to hear
from the other beds
in the small dark room.

Under the blankets,
her back to us
and her face to the unshaded window,
she recited the petitions
she'd learned as a child—

Give us this day our daily bread . . .
I pray the Lord my soul to keep . . .

and then, like a child
she'd begin to bless
generations of kin.

Bless Marian
Bless Robert and Billy
*   Bless Nancy and Susan*
*   Debbie and Todd . . .*

Who's she trying to impress?
my brother asked with youthful disdain.
Well I don't mind, so shush!
I said
lying quite still
as I listened for my name.

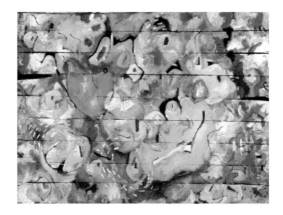

God Enjoys Itself

Tom Block, USA

INFLUENCE: JUDAISM, SUFISM (ORIGINAL: SECULARISM)

The God I Know

Sibusisiwe Nkomo, USA (birthplace: Zimbabwe)

INFLUENCE: SKEPTICISM (ORIGINAL: CHRISTIANITY)

Hi God
I know I haven't spoken to You for a while
But that is because everything was going so well.
Now Suku tells me that my mother is dying,
I guess You felt that I needed to get in touch with
    You,
So that's why I'm talking to You today.

TUMIN, CHINA—TWO NORTH KOREAN MINISTERS WHO REGULARLY CROSS INTO THEIR COUNTRY DESPITE CERTAIN DEATH IF THEY ARE CAUGHT TRYING TO SPREAD THE GOSPEL TO THEIR FELLOW BRETHREN.

Faith Enough for All North Korean Missionaries in China #4

Nayan Sthankiya, Canada (birthplace: Uganda)
INFLUENCE: BUDDHISM (ORIGINAL: HINDUISM)

Breathe

Peggy Heinrich, USA
INFLUENCE: SPIRITUALITY

The moment I think
I've done it
meaning wordlessness
the words
fill empty mind
thought explodes
through hard-won empty space

The meditation bench
warms with effort
to be effortless
a trying time

relax, relax
the words disturb
whatever makes up mind

Observe the breath
enter, leave
something's
breathing me
this quiet time of day.

Shadow

Ayo Oyeku, Nigeria

INFLUENCE: SPIRITUALITY, HEAVENLY INSPIRATION

Your feel dazzles me
And I hear a drop
From my leaf
Into that stream . . .
   Your cool breeze
   Blows and mumbles gently
And I feel it in my inner . . .

Then I draw
From the stream of life
Then a dark transparent figure
Falls on my source
And behold it was a shadow
   Yet I do not see
But perhaps it was you . . .

And so I set out at dawn
And behold your shadow
Was waiting by the stream
Then my *second* stretches
   Forth on this flow
   And your shadow held
   Mine on this stream . . .
Though I never saw your coat

So, hand in hand
We walked on this stream
With your shadow on mine
   Though this stream
   Separates us both
But together we go . . .

Farming Faith: A South Korean Minister's Calling #4

Nayan Sthankiya, Canada (birthplace: Uganda)

INFLUENCE: BUDDHISM (ORIGINAL: HINDUISM)

River

Kathy Putnam, USA

this river of air slides
around me through me in
me around me through me
in me river of life within
me through me around me
flowing lifting my hair lifting
my skirt lifting my
eyes

as long as life as
short as breath always
twirling whirling neverending
mother gratitude fills my
eyes and i cry thank you
thank you thank
you for the great
river

Shine

Janet Baker, USA

INFLUENCE: SPIRITUALITY, YOGA, SHAMANISM, MEDITATION
(ORIGINAL: ROMAN CATHOLICISM)

To shine is to be god is to be clear blue sky is to be enough.
And night is the time the shine is held by stars in the blackness.

And I can allow that god is the same as shine
since the beginning of my tribe, and I can imagine shine
as the god I dance for, and I might imagine during night
with no blue sky the moon glow shines softer.

I am dancing my words around the church, shaking myself at Christ,
I am dancing sex and shimmers, dancing sweat and glisten,
and since Christ is a man, he shines at the dancer,
slips money in her belt, dances his hips into hers round the room.

No need to harden shine into solid gold of Buddha, no need to climb
skyward to be closer, carry prayers to the highest mountain
to be closer, so the Hindus have blue-skinned gods to remind
how blue disappears each night returns each day.

If blue sky enters my heart, this dance will be enough,
blue sky shining with no need for my own words, blue
beyond the need to word, beyond the need to poetry. Shine
this god of the beginning of my tribe when god and shine were one.

Anima Rising

Vandorn Hinnant, USA

INFLUENCE: SPIRITUALITY

Wax Paper

J. D. Smith, USA

INFLUENCE: CHRISTIANITY, BUDDHISM (ORIGINAL: EASTERN & WESTERN CHRISTIANITY)

If things could be patron saints, I would take as mine wax paper. Gold would have too many devotees, a backlog of petitions. Air would accompany my every step, even if I asked for nothing, even into dark corners and far countries where I might seek the privacy to sin. But wax paper is only as ubiquitous as it needs to be. Name a town where it can't be had if you open your heart to the effort of finding it at a decent hour, maybe any hour, in a pantry or a drawer or, in America, in a cabinet beneath a sink, rolled hard by a J-curved pipe. Or if you open your wallet by a mere crack.

How many martyrs have baked against metal simply to increase another's joy by as little as a cookie or a cinnamon roll, and held fast till their work is done? Adjacent sugars recant, caramelized, or fall away into apostate ash. A trial by water that would render dissolute even the salt of the earth fails to abrade a sheet that has maintained its opposition to all friction in the face of serrated strips and vindictive scissors, and at the hands of men. They could wear themselves out and shred every roll in a shipment, and they would have for their effort confetti in one color, that of waxed paper. The merest tatter could resist a butter-glistening croissant, remain impervious to the oregano-flecked current of olive oil escaping from between a slice of provolone and a torpedo roll.

Even the forces and principalities of french fries and fried chicken, onion rings and rings of calamari, shall not prevail against the smallest scrap. What object of veneration could provide a worthier example? Nothing could more firmly keep and preserve novenas, or accept messages of thanks for favors granted in the classifieds. San Saran, San Papel de Cera, *ora pro nobis*, in this too, too porous flesh.

Frammento

Escha van den Bogerd,
The Netherlands
INFLUENCE: SPIRITUALITY, TRAVEL

Cosmic Zen Ballet

Michael Meyerhofer, USA
INFLUENCE: ZEN BUDDHISM (ORIGINAL: ROMAN CATHOLICISM)

Fill a cup with water
and then break it,

the water spills
but does not disappear.

It may soak the floor,
the earth, may evaporate

but will eventually return
to the clouds

and become water again.
Even the universe expands

and contracts
like a pulsing heart

over trillions of years,
scattering seeds

from which the galaxies sprout
and spread, then

rush back together.
Life itself wheels

and dies then is born
again, like the stars,

coming and going
in a cosmic ballet

and God did not start this.
God does not end this.

God is the ballet.

Foxes

Christopher Woods, USA

INFLUENCE: SPIRITUALITY

Running with them
For a time
I
once divided
Into weeks
Is like a river that never dries
But goes
and goes, coasting
Over shells and sand beds,
The souls of mountains
Breaking up, migrating.
Being among them
Nights
in

frostbound
fields
Beneath a ghost moon haze,
I need to believe
They too
are counting stars
And all the time between them.

Heaven

Nancy Shiffrin, USA

INFLUENCE: JUDAISM

A squirrel scavenges breadcrusts
at the corner café.
I turn
and watch two petals
detach
from a full-blown rose.
Lustrous pink, edged with wine, white at the
    center,
they drift down
the fragile afternoon breeze.
The squirrel scurries to the top of a palm tree,
his treasure clenched between his teeth.
In the blinding summer chill,
for just one moment,
my chattering mind is silent.

A Place for Thinking

Paul Cernak, USA

List of Contributors

Further information about contributors, including links to their websites, can be found at www.IlluminationsBook.com.

"A craft can only have meaning when it serves a spiritual way."

—TITUS BURKHARDT

ACKNOWLEDGMENTS

We wish to thank the following individuals for their invaluable feedback, support, and assistance with this project and with various drafts of the manuscript: Stacy Aab, Jamie Boone, Vince Gowmon, Shalini Jain, Stacey Lawson, Colin McLin, Susanna McMahon, Jennifer Langston McGee, Natalie Michael, and Catherine Watson.

Mary Tompkins provided assistance above and beyond the call of duty, from helping gather interview respondents worldwide to her incredible work organizing submissions. Larry Tompkins and Bridget Tomlinson supported her in these efforts.

We are indebted to Chris Wright for generously creating the website and Michael Boyd, John P. Courtney, and others at Andrews Kurth LLP for offering legal help and advice. Thanks also to Joseph Guglietti Design for producing a beautiful sample of the book.

Ian Sobieski, Rev. Howard E. Caesar, and Arielle Ford provided assistance and introductions that were instrumental to the project.

A special thanks to Julie Bennett at Ten Speed Press and to our agent, Sally van Haitsma of the Castiglia Literary Agency, for their enthusiasm, belief in the book, and efforts to get it to publication. We are grateful for the tremendous creativity and patience Nancy Austin provided in her design work for the book.

Copyright © 2006 by Mark L. Tompkins

Each piece is copyrighted by the individual contributor as credited in the List of Contributors on pages 144–45, and is gratefully used with the permission of the artist or writer.

Front cover photo: "Examiner" by Gina Glover
Back cover art: "Three Golden Rings" by Vandorn Hinnant

CA

Celestial Arts
an imprint of Ten Speed Press
Box 7123
Berkeley, California 94707
www.tenspeed.com

Distributed in Australia by Simon and Schuster Australia, in Canada by Ten Speed Press Canada, in New Zealand by Southern Publishers Group, in South Africa by Real Books, and in the United Kingdom and Europe by Publishers Group UK.

Cover and text design by Nancy Austin

Library of Congress Cataloging-in-Publication

Illuminations : expressions of the personal spiritual experience / edited by Mark L. Tompkins and Jennifer McMahon.
    p. cm.
  Summary: "A collection of interviews, original artworks, photographs, poems, and short prose pieces that express the personal spiritual experiences of more than 180 contributors from 43 countries representing a diverse range of faiths and traditions"--Provided by publisher.
  Includes index.
  ISBN-13: 978-1-58761-277-0
  ISBN-10: 1-58761-277-1
  1. Spiritual life--Miscellanea. 2. Spiritual biography. I. Tompkins, Mark L. II. McMahon, Jennifer. III. Title.

  BL624.I45 2006
  204'.2--dc22

  2006011187

Printed in Singapore
First printing, 2006
1 2 3 4 5 6 7 8 9 10 — 10 09 08 07 06